# Heroes Alongside Us

# Heroes Alongside Us

One Man's Tale of Unlikely Success
and the Men Who Made it Possible

*Eric F. Rieseberg*

# Heroes Alongside Us

"If you ever doubted the importance of heroes in your life, then the effect these five men had on Eric Rieseberg's life story will be convincing enough. There is truth in the pages of this very wise, compelling and well-told story. The guidelines Eric has used in his life can help us to define our own heroes and even perhaps to become one. This book is an excellent guide in the search for personal happiness and success."

—Jan Cousteau
Co-founder, EarthEcho International
Author, Environmentalist
Washington, D.C.

"Eric's book served as a catalyst, making me think of the numerous people who have helped me along the way. Many of the events he described, both in high school and throughout his career, are vivid reminders that we've all had people who have influenced us—both positively and negatively. Calling those with a positive influence "heroes" is a wonderful way to consider their impact. I have known and worked with for Eric for over thirty years. Funny, based on his definition, I would call Eric one of my heroes. *Heroes Alongside Us* is an easy and thoroughly enjoyable read."

—Peter A. Hofstetter, FACHE
Chief Executive Officer, Taos Health Systems, Inc.
Taos, NM

"*Heroes Alongside Us* outlines all of the qualities needed to build a happy personal life and successful business. As a healthcare professional, United States Military Academy graduate and U.S. Army Colonel, I relate closely to Eric Rieseberg's values, skills, and discipline. Having known and worked with him for twenty-three years, he is old school, driven, and demanding of himself and others. A number of his business subordinates, whom he coached and mentored, learned the value of being accountable for their actions and achieving results far beyond their previously experienced limits. As a result, many have gone on to jobs with increased responsibility and success."

—Brian F. Wells
Colonel, U.S. Army Reserve (Retired)
Tampa, FL

"Read this book and I guarantee that you will identify with one or more of the people in it, as well as discover how to deal with life's challenges. Eric has portrayed heroes with whom 'regular' people can identify: coaches who have to make tough decisions and teach their players about what real life is all about; a courageous woman battling a devastating disease; a couple enduring heartbreak beyond measure with the loss of a child. He demonstrates that being a real hero is not being an All-American lacrosse player; rather, it is being an ordinary person called upon to do extraordinary things—because those things simply have to be done."

—Robert J. Rule
High School Teammate of Eric F. Rieseberg
National Lacrosse Hall of Fame Member
Manhasset, NY

"Timeless in its message, *Heroes Alongside Us* is a must-read treatise for any 18- to 25-year-old positioning themselves to launch their career. For those of us in youth development, education, and business, Eric Rieseberg's personal story and call to action is fresh and inspiring— a reminder that we can make a crucial difference in the trajectory of young people."

–Mat Levine
Founder of CityLax and Doc's NYC Lacrosse
New York, NY

"Buy this book and read it. You will learn, love it, and not be able to put it down. Eric Rieseberg extracts the lessons of a life of hardship turned into a life of contribution and success. The key? His everyday role models, mentors, and heroes: individuals who came alongside him, bringing him to a place where he can make sense of it all, and teach us the lessons he learned on the way about integrity, hard work, doing for others, and living nobly. Thanks to them, Eric wrote *Heroes Alongside Us*. He is now one of the heroes alongside me."

—Henry Fishman M.D.
Washington, D.C.

*Heroes Alongside Us* is the inspirational story of Eric Rieseberg's life journey, and how those he defines as heroes impacted him with their noble acts of unselfish giving. These heroes ultimately brought out the hidden potential in Eric that some educators failed to recognize. This book defines how ordinary people are capable of bettering the lives of others, and it motivated me to look at my own life's journey and identify my heroes."

—Joseph Capela
Manhasset Lacrosse Hall of Fame
Chatham, NJ

Salt Island Publishing
28370 Terrazza Lane
Naples, FL 34110

www.HeroesAlongsideUs.com

ISBN: 978-0692242261

Printed in the United States of America
First Printing 2014

*Cover design by*
Alexander Von Ness

*Interior design by*
Nand Kishore Pandey

*Interior portrait drawings by*
Jeff Sorg

Author photo taken at the South Carolina Yacht Club

# CONTENTS

# Foreword

On a wintry Sunday afternoon over forty years ago, I was driving by the Manhasset, New York High School where I coached lacrosse, when I noticed someone practicing against an outside wall of the school. It was Eric Rieseberg. There he was—all alone—practicing his skills, not only for his own benefit, but also because he didn't want to disappoint his new friends and teammates. Eric's working to hone his skills that day turned out to be exemplary of how he would live his life: with focus and discipline, always a team player, and ultimately successfully.

Eric is far from the first to have been shaped by lacrosse. The sport may well be the oldest team sport in America, with its heritage dating back to Native Americans who played the sport—known as the Creator's game—many centuries ago. Hundreds of men played against each other and the games often lasted for days. Lacrosse was a sport of brotherly love and enabled the players to compete against one another with the utmost respect.

Eric and I lost touch for several decades and reconnected when he came to visit me in Ithaca, New York last year. We had a great time getting caught up on the last forty years. I was saddened to learn about the hardships Eric has endured, and so pleased to hear of his success. There is no doubt in my mind that Eric's success is partially due to the personal foundation he formed when he played lacrosse in high school. Those who play lacrosse learn a number of principles and values early on:

- Always look your opponent in the eye.
- Be accountable.
- Assist your team in achieving success.
- Play your best with strong desire.
- Exhibit good sportsmanship.
- Respect others.

- Be aggressive, yet in control.
- Lead by example.
- Seek and reach your goal.

I'm proud to be able to say that over the course of my career I've witnessed how the principles and values learned in the game of lacrosse have positively impacted not only Eric's life, but the lives of countless men: I've stayed in close contact with many of my players over the years, and have seen them move on from success at Manhasset High School and Cornell University to successful careers as doctors, veterinarians, corporate executives, lawyers, teachers, college professors, and a four-star general in the United States Marine Corps. Not only are these men successful in their careers, but they are leaders in their communities; they are giving, caring, and sharing.

In sports over the centuries there have been many athletes who were not superstars, but who one day rose to the occasion to help their team win—because they had exceptional desire. And, in fact, it's the ordinary lacrosse player who makes a team highly successful. The average player who doesn't have the speed or agility of his teammates must rise to the occasion and bring forth everything he has to help his team be successful.

And so it is with life: The ordinary people with exceptional desire rise to the occasion. Eric uses his own story to demonstrate how success is possible for anyone, regardless of the odds.

Richie Moran
Ithaca, New York

# A Note to My Readers

vividly remember the first time: My face hitting the ground with a thud. The taste and smell of grass combined with dirt. And then, just as quickly as I had hit the ground, one of my teammates helped me up so I could run again. I spit the dirt and grass out of my mouth, and kept on going. It was my first face plant.

As a lacrosse player I learned the importance of getting up quickly when I fell face-first into the grass, or got knocked on my butt. Falling and getting up again—*fast*: That's what a successful life is all about—and it's also what this book is about. I believe in order to be successful, we must experience failure and learn how to get up, brush ourselves off, and get moving again ... occasionally with assistance from others. It's when you've fallen—and tasted the dirt and grass—that you decide you don't care for their taste, and that you must work harder, stronger, better and faster to ensure you don't continue to eat the grass and dirt life may have in store for you.

I've had my share of face plants, literally and figuratively. Growing up, the odds were, perhaps, stacked against me: I was a sub-par student from a dysfunctional family. Yet, I believe by anyone's standards, I'm considered successful. How? ... Why? *My heroes.* I've been blessed to have five men in my life, my heroes, to whom I attribute my ability to recover from my many face plants. Each of my heroes came along at a tipping point in my life, and helped me overcome the odds and change the outcome

that might have been. This book is the story of how my heroes changed my life—and how heroes can change yours. It's also about how you, as a hero, can change the lives of others.

My hope for you, my reader, is that you will see yourself in my story and take some sort of action: Perhaps you, too, have endured more face plants than you'd like, and are in need of a hero. Seek one out! But, remember to choose wisely. Or, you may discover that you are already a hero in the eyes of someone you've helped up, and if not … perhaps you'll be inspired to become one.

Eric Rieseberg

**CHAPTER ONE**

# Obstacles from the Start

I was happy … for a few minutes. The sun was bright and warmed my skin as I walked home from school after lacrosse practice. I looked up at the trees with their new leaves: There was a slight breeze that caused the leaves to do a happy dance.

I opened the front door of our two-story house. Though the sun was blinding in the blue spring sky, inside our house it was dark as night: In every area of the house, the room-darkening shades had been pulled all the way down to the window sills. The drapes were drawn tightly closed, without so much as a tiny opening where they met in the middle of the window. Not a single window was open; the house seemed totally devoid of air. It was silent: no whirring sound of the washing machine or dishwasher. This didn't strike me as anything odd: It was just like many other afternoons when I got home from school. I simply assumed that Mom hadn't gotten out of bed yet. In fact, it was rare for her to be up and about when I got home from school. Sometimes she still wasn't up at 6 p.m. From where I stood at the front door, I could see last night's pots and pans filling the sink and dirty dishes scattered on the counter— along with an empty bourbon bottle. A single glass, with an inch or so of watered-down whiskey left in it, was still on the coffee table in the living

1

room. It wasn't unusual for me to see a couple of highball glasses—still sporting tiny bits of ice—on the living room coffee table when I left for school in the morning. When I saw those highball glasses with remnants of drinks from just a few hours before, I knew something was wrong.

As the oldest child by quite a few years, and a son at that, I always felt as though it was my responsibility to take control and fix whatever was wrong.

As ill as she was, my mom was wonderful in so many ways. I loved her and never once doubted her love for me, though, from a young age, I somehow understood that she didn't have the ability to really show it. My dad was a four-striped captain in the United States Navy. Many people considered him to be a brilliant man. It was highly unusual to make it to captain, never having gone to Annapolis. The Navy even sent him to Harvard Business School, as one of only two candidates sent to Harvard that year for an MBA. At age forty-four, after twenty-two years in the Navy, my dad went on to become the vice president of a large shipping company, Grace Lines, in New York City.

Dad was mostly absent—if not physically, then emotionally. We moved seven times—pretty much every two or three years, and sometimes more often—while I was growing up. Mom and Dad didn't get along, but Mom played the role of a Navy captain's wife quite well, even in spite of her illness. My parents were always attending parties in Washington D. C. and Mom excelled in that capacity. In fact, they attended parties wherever we lived. Mom was stunning, truly drop-dead gorgeous. She looked just like one of those old black and white photos of a Hollywood movie star that anyone would look at and say, "She's beautiful." At parties, people were automatically drawn to her, I suppose for many reasons: she was attractive and charming, and she was the wife of a senior naval officer. I thought she was gifted with a wonderful personality and tremendous charisma, and at the same time, she was also high maintenance. In my young mind, I believed she thought she was a bit of a queen, a chosen one. My feelings about my mom were confirmed later in life by those who knew her. Mom went to college for a short time, and then married Dad, a naval ensign from a well-known Washington, D.C. family. Mom and Dad had a big military wedding, complete with swords and white uniforms, and all the pomp and circumstance.

When I saw it was dark in the house on that spring afternoon, I flicked on a lamp that sat on a table next to the front door. *Will things ever change? Will it always be like this?* I had to keep my mom's illness a secret from my friends. I couldn't be what I thought I wanted to be (the "big man on campus") and tell the truth about my mom. I couldn't go around telling my friends that my mom was mentally ill, an alcoholic, and an abuser of prescription drugs. I couldn't divulge the fact that my mom commonly drank too much, that she often couldn't get up in the morning and make lunch for her kids like every other mom, and sometimes, when she did finally wake up, she had the smell of vomit on her nightgown.

I felt so alone. I *was* alone.

Out of the corner of my eye, I caught a glimpse of my mom on the second floor. She was running down the hall, her nightgown billowing out behind her. Within a few seconds, a number of scenarios flashed through my brain. I bounded up the stairs, taking them three at a time. My heart was pounding in my chest as I went from one room to the next looking for my mother. And then I found her. I stood in the doorway of the bathroom for a second, almost paralyzed.

"STOP, Mom STOP!" I screamed at the top of my lungs. *No! Could this really be happening?*

Mom was holding one of those large amber pill bottles in her right hand. In a split second, she managed to snap off the secured white cap, put her mouth around the bottle, and start chugging. I rushed into the bathroom.

"Mom, DON'T," I screamed again.

It was as if she couldn't hear me. I knocked the bottle out of her hand and hit her hard across the side of her face in an attempt to bring her out of her stupor.

"Spit them out," I begged.

Again, no response. I grabbed her cheek and shook until the pills fell out of her mouth and onto the floor. Mom looked up at me; her eyes were full of fear and sadness. She slowly made her way back to her bedroom and closed the door behind her. I picked up all the pills that were on the floor and flushed them down the toilet.

The fact that my mom tried to kill herself right in front of me was never spoken about. I had to get up and go to school the next morning and perform on the lacrosse field that afternoon—as if nothing had happened. This wasn't the first time I had to deal with stormy seas, and shock in my life, and it certainly wouldn't be the last. And, this trauma was far from the only obstacle that I would have to overcome.

## CHAPTER TWO

# The Key to Success

When it came to academics, I was certainly not a success—by any definition. I'd had a poor foundation: By the time I reached high school, I'd attended seven different schools. My parents never saw an A on my report card. Not once. I simply wasn't a studious kid and didn't apply myself. I was never book-smart, and didn't particularly enjoy studying or my textbooks—even when I opened them. I loved to read, but not textbooks. In my early years, academic mediocrity, failure and I became very well acquainted.

Manhasset is a hamlet on the North Shore of Long Island, New York. Appropriately nicknamed "the Gold Coast," the North Shore is well-known for its affluence and elegance, the Nelson DeMille novels that take place there, and the many rich and famous who have called it home.

Wealth isn't the only thing Manhasset was—and is—known for: Manhasset High School has always consistently ranked in the top one hundred high schools in the country, and the year I entered Manhasset High, it was ranked in the top ten. And there I was: a non-academic young man who was suddenly injected into one of the best high schools in America.

Toward the end of my junior year, my parents received a call from Mrs. Crane, one of the guidance counselors, who requested that my parents come to the school to meet with her and Mr. Single, her boss. Mr. Single was the head of the guidance department and he knew me well—I was never really in trouble or a trouble maker, but often on the periphery of it, similar to "where there's smoke there's fire." Call me smoke!

"Your son Eric isn't living up to his potential. He's not going to make it," Mrs. Crane authoritatively told Mom and Dad.

"I suggest Eric apply to a vocational school and become a welder or an air conditioning repairman," she continued.

There's certainly nothing wrong with a vocational career, but I wonder if Mrs. Crane realized she was talking to a Harvard MBA, ex-military guy who undoubtedly had high aspirations for his eldest child.

Flash forward nearly forty years: My best friend from high school and I visited Manhasset High. It was during the Christmas holiday break, so school wasn't in session, but the front doors were open. As we walked down the main corridor, that familiar "school smell" permeated my nostrils. I searched for my locker, found it, and just stared at it. I was nudged back to the present by the faint sound of someone typing. We walked around the corner toward the administrative offices where a woman was feverishly tapping her fingers on her computer keyboard. I glanced at the name plate on the door. It read "Superintendent of Schools, Mr. Single." The administrative assistant looked up from her work.

"Happy holidays. May I help you?" she inquired.

"Is Mr. Single around?" I asked.

"No, I'm sorry. He's away on holiday," she replied.

We turned to leave when the administrative assistant asked, "I'll let Mr. Single know you were here. Who should I say stopped by?"

I answered, "Tell Mr. Single that Eric Rieseberg was here."

"Is there a message?" she asked.

I paused for a moment and then chuckled, "Tell him things worked out much better than he would have thought."

Yes, things certainly did turn out much better: at age twenty-six, I became the youngest CEO in a company that managed fifty hospitals. By the age of thirty-two, I'd enjoyed not one, but three CEO-ships. At the age of thirty-four, I was in charge of twenty hospitals. I achieved my goal of retiring at age fifty. (Huge mistake.) I'd say that by anyone's standards, I've been quite successful in my life.

And by the way, my mom and dad never told me about the meeting with Mrs. Crane. In fact, it wasn't until I was around forty years old that my dad divulged the secret meeting with my high school guidance counselor. He told me the story in his usual way, completely devoid of any emotion. Though when he finished, I detected a glimmer in his eye as he said, "It's a good thing we didn't listen to her."

So, how did I, a chubby, never-got-picked-for-any-team, sub-par student from a dysfunctional family end up having things work out much better than Mr. Single—or anyone for that matter—would have thought?

One word: HEROES. I couldn't have done it without them. My heroes were the key to my success, and a big part of the reason I'm writing this book.

### What is Success?

Success looks different for each of us. However, I believe if you were to query one hundred people as to their definition of success, you would get one hundred definitions that are all quite similar. Further, if you were to ask those same people to name the top ten characteristics of success, I believe everyone would have similar components on their lists. The bottom line is that success is very similar in the views of most people.

The Merriam-Webster dictionary defines success as "the fact of getting or achieving wealth, respect, or fame." In my view, it's not enough to say someone is successful because of the amount of money in their bank account. We live in a very materialistic society: For many, financial achievement equals success. I think (particularly in America) we are bringing up our kids with the idea that they need to make a big hit financially, and that's their ticket to success. That is absolutely wrong. I've lived it. I've been there.

Likewise, it's not enough to say the achievement of fame equals success. Hitler was famous—and I suppose he was also successful: He achieved his goals, as horrific as they were. Hitler's achievements do not equate to success in my mind.

My definition of success is a simple one, yet it takes the concept of success to a higher level:

- Success is the achievement of a pre-determined, *noble* goal.

I'm not talking kings and queens, or blue-blooded aristocrats here. Noble goals are generous, good-hearted and well-meant. A noble action is something you do to help others rather than yourself. Those who accomplish noble goals typically have ideals and patterns of behavior that lead to a successful life and help their fellow man.

My mom—and probably yours, too—always used to tell me, "Choose your friends carefully." I didn't pay any attention to her warnings as a kid, but I know now that she was absolutely right: If you want to be successful, hook your wagon to someone who has established a pattern of achieving pre-determined, noble goals.

Learn from and be influenced by the best: *Hook your wagon to a hero.*

## CHAPTER THREE

# Getting the Best and the Worst

With Dad in the military, we moved every two to three years. The constant moving meant always having to leave my friends and forge new relationships in the next location—not something I relished even if I was pretty good at it. There were always the cliques that had to be broken into … or not.

My parent's dysfunctional marriage didn't help matters any. They lived apart for two months, and then got back together to "try again." When they were together, they fought constantly and so would separate again, sometimes for as long as six months. The dysfunction in their marriage ultimately reached the major league category.

It was my hero, Tom, who provided my only refuge in my younger years. (More about Tom in Chapter Six.)

My dad was mostly a non-communicative, military guy. He was the son of a single woman, raised during the depression. Grandma Rieseberg wasn't just *any* woman: When she was sixteen years old, she eloped with some guy from Washington D.C. The couple fled to New York City and lived there until they were finally found by a private investigator who'd been hired by Grandma Rieseberg's brothers and sisters. As the story goes, Grandma's family literally extracted her from the arms of this fellow, and brought her back to Washington to straighten her out. I guess Grandma Rieseberg was a bit wild. She eventually married Lieutenant Harry E. Rieseberg, one of the earliest undersea hard-helmet divers in the United States. They had one child, my dad, and divorced after only a year. Harry was married four more times ... I understand I have cousins all across America. My dad never knew his father, nor did I, but I've enjoyed getting to know Harry by reading the dozen books he wrote about his undersea exploits. Grandma Rieseberg was someone very special: a hard-working woman who single-handedly raised a son, my dad—who ultimately became very successful.

Up until the age of six, I was an only child, and then my two brothers came along, two years apart. I don't remember much about my relationship with my dad when I was very young, probably because he was never around. I do recall, however, having disagreements with him— and not understanding him—starting when I was five or six years old. These weren't the typical five-year-old-versus-dad-why-can't-we-go-fishing-today disagreements. I wonder today what my dad must have thought of me when, at five years old, I would ask, "Dad, why do you act that way?" There was always a dearth of empathy, a stoic disciplined air, and zero positive feedback. I felt no matter how good I was, it was never good enough. My wonderful Aunt Jean, my mom's sister, always said I was the beneficiary of the best and the worst of my parents. I was the beneficiary of the best and most normal years my parents had together, but as the eldest child, I was the son who had to deal with the worst part of my mother's life. I know I got the best compared with my brothers, who only saw the worst. I don't know if mom and dad were ever happy together, but ever since I was old enough to be thinking about it, their marriage was deteriorating. The absolute best years for me were when we were living in Maine. My dad had been transferred again: He was now second in command at the Portsmouth (New Hampshire) Naval Shipyard and we lived just a few minutes away in Kittery, Maine. It was the mid-1950s. I remember playing catch with Dad a few times in the backyard, and going fishing once with him—and Mom baking Christmas cookies. And, one of my younger brothers was born in Kittery. My parents probably weren't doing well from a marital standpoint: I could often hear arguments long into the night.

When I was seven years old, we were transferred to London, and that's when their marriage completely eroded. Mom was probably dealing with post-partum depression from the birth of my youngest brother; my dad was traveling a lot, and his work weighed heavily on her. I think Mom was lonely. When Dad was around, they were always attending embassy parties that were well-known for their abundance of alcohol.

As an eight-year-old, I knew that my dad was stationed at the United States Embassy in Grosvenor Square as a supply officer and naval attaché; however, I didn't really know what it meant to be either one of those things. I do remember Dad talking casually with one of his embassy colleagues one day, and saying something about the Russian spies who were parked right outside the embassy gates—apparently a common occurrence. I never gave it a second thought.

It was perhaps fifteen years after I graduated from college that I finally learned exactly what Dad did in the Navy: I was living in upstate New York and needed a new television. I drove into town and saw the United States flag and a Navy Ensign flag flying outside the local electronics store; so, I parked, walked in, and started chatting with the owner.

"I noticed your Navy Ensign flag outside," I said.

"Yes, I recruit for the Navy," he replied.

"My dad was in the Navy: He was a supply officer in London at the embassy and then he worked on naval communications systems," I responded, and went on to describe what I knew of Dad's work.

"Sounds like a spy to me," was the response.

You could have knocked me over with a feather.

I saw my dad a couple weeks later and mentioned to him that I'd had an unusual conversation with the owner of our local electronics store.

"Were you a spy?" I asked my dad, trying to be nonchalant.

"Oh sure," he answered. Then he spilled his guts regarding his long-term relationship with the United States National Security Agency.

As I think of it now, my dad had the perfect makeup to be a spy: he was a non-compelling communicator who never showed emotion. He was always rather distant, disenfranchised, and aloof, and not particularly interested in anything. I learned that day that Dad's work as a supply officer was nothing more than a front for his work with the National Security Agency (NSA). He had set up the radio and electronic communication systems in the Pentagon and was sent to London to do the same thing all over Europe for NATO.

I have three distinct memories from our time in London: I got dressed every morning in my gray flannel shorts, necktie, blazer and a baseball cap before making my way to the American School in London. I came home at the end of the school day, often to find my mother in bed. I only thought my mom slept a lot: The notion that a mom might be drinking too much isn't something that enters the mind of an eight-year-old. After school, my friends and I would make our way to Hempstead Heath— then a very rustic city park—where we played war and killed the enemy by the hundreds. Our enemies at the time were the Nazis. Today, children fight different enemies.

And I remember an embassy party, one to which children were invited, though most parents didn't bring their children. I went to the party with Dad, who went in full military dress. There must have been two hundred people, everyone all dressed up, holding cocktails in one hand and using the other hand to enhance their conversation. The gigantic room buzzed incessantly with the chatter of their voices. I was standing next to Dad when very suddenly, all conversation stopped. I looked up to see every head turning in the same direction; as heads turned, mouths dropped open. I looked to see what could possibly have brought all the conversation to a halt. And as a nine-year-old, my mouth dropped open too: descending the spiral staircase was the most beautiful woman I had ever set my young eyes on. Her beauty was almost matched by her stunning gown, which was the most gorgeous color I had ever seen.

The woman was my mom.

Time seemed to stop for several seconds as my mom walked down the stairs, all eyes upon her. The fabric for mom's gown, a brilliant turquoise streaked with veins of gold, came from India. The bolt of fabric had been a gift from Shala, the wife of one of Dad's colleagues at Harvard, and my mom had the dress custom-designed. That moment is one of my most vivid childhood memories.

After London, we moved back to Washington, and I started fourth grade. My dad had multiple assignments in Washington D.C. over a five-year period, including jobs at the Pentagon and Ward Circle. In September of 1963, Dad decided he would retire from the Navy at the end of the year, and we would move for the last time—to Manhasset, New York. Our final move held great promise for me. My parents' marriage was on the brink of disaster. All the moving had taken its toll on my mom and she had started to develop manic-depression. I secretly prayed that our last move would be the medicine that made things normal again. It would be different this time: Dad would have a new job, he'd be home more, and we'd all be together. Mom and Dad agreed to give their marriage one more try. The move represented the opportunity for a fresh start and new beginning ... great hope and optimism for all of us.

I'd always been overweight, and I decided it was time for a new beginning for me, too: I would no longer be the last guy to be picked for basketball. I made a commitment to myself to lose weight before we moved and I had to make new friends—yet again. As I think back on it, my desire to lose weight probably had as much to do with wanting to kiss girls as it did with making new guy friends and getting picked for basketball or some other sport.

I entered Manhasset High in January of ninth grade, a relatively good-looking kid at six feet two inches tall, weighing two hundred ten pounds, about twenty pounds less than I had weighed a few months earlier. My hard work paid off: Not only did I get to kiss a lot of girls, but my new friends asked if I'd ever played lacrosse. They assumed I had since I came from the Washington D.C./Maryland area, but I'd never even held a lacrosse stick in my hand and knew next to nothing about the game. They suggested I try out for the ninth grade junior varsity team. It was at the first round of tryouts that my second hero, Richie Moran, entered my life.

## CHAPTER FOUR

# What is a Hero?

The combination of a dad who was rarely there and a mom who was emotionally ill with episodic bouts of alcoholism made for a dysfunctional family life—to say the least. Add failure after failure on my part, and the result wasn't exactly an equation for success. My first tastes of success, and the success I continued to enjoy throughout my life, were because of my heroes. I know that now—looking back decades later—but I'm certain it's not something I thought about as a young child or even as a teenager.

So, what is a hero? Of course we have heroes as the main characters in books and movies, but that's not the kind of hero I'm talking about. If I may refer to Mr. Webster once again: A hero is "a person who is admired for great or brave acts or fine qualities," or "a person who is greatly admired." My heroes were all this and more.

Here's my definition of a hero:

> A hero is an individual who, through noble actions—and patterns of achieving pre-determined noble goals over a protracted period of time—has improved the lives of those who have become associated with or influenced by him or her.

As with my definition of *success*, the word *noble* plays a key role in my definition of a hero. (Noble means generous, good-hearted, and well-meant. A noble action is something that is done to help others rather than to help oneself.) Heroes come in different packages: They don't look alike; their noble actions and patterns of achieving goals are not the same. However, all my heroes have a great deal in common and are successful by anyone's definition.

*Hero versus Celebrity*

In today's culture, if you're really rich or really popular, then often you're a celebrity. Achieving wealth and fame may make you a celebrity, but it won't necessarily make you successful, nor will it make you a hero. Will hooking your wagon to a celebrity—or even emulating that celebrity—make you successful? No. Celebrities often surround themselves with enablers, people who underpin their celebrity, and tell them what they want to hear in order to preserve their relationship with this individual who has achieved fame and fortune. Michael Jackson was an absolute talent. Unfortunately, he surrounded himself with enablers—who were not willing to risk themselves, their place in life, or their careers—instead of with heroes. Celebrities often surround themselves with those who will tell them what they want to hear as opposed to heroes, who would intercede regardless of the celebrity's reaction.

In my youth, I met famous and powerful people in the military, the government, and industry. Intuitively and by trial and error, I learned from an early age that just because someone is famous, a celebrity, or rich, doesn't mean they are a hero, a success, or even someone worth associating with. In fact, it's often just the opposite.

We are often looking for a fast way up or out, especially when it comes to money: I've met quite a few young people who seem to want others to provide for them. Get-rich-quick schemes abound; thousands of individuals have made money on the Internet selling programs on how to get rich on the Internet. Other so-called gurus have gone the way of selling get-rich-quick schemes—from flipping houses to getting free money to pay your bills—via television infomercials. Celebrity is equivalent to the fast way out or up.

The youth of today surround themselves with celebrity—via social media and by watching television. A friend recently told me about her niece, who apparently has hooked her wagon to a certain celebrity. The niece was out of a job and couldn't pay her rent. Yet, every day she purchased a $6-per-can drink from her local health food store, because a certain celebrity touted the benefits of that drink. Likewise, this unemployed young woman bought a very expensive pair of boots (on a credit card), because this same celebrity wears similar boots.

Those around us whom we choose as our heroes are not always the ones who have been tested, by time and outcome, to qualify them as the type of individual after whom we should model our lives. At times, those who are viewed as shining stars are, in reality, not shining stars at all. Sometimes the closer we look, the more flaws we become aware of.

To whom do you want to hook your wagon? A celebrity, whose fame and fortune you admire from afar and are unlikely to rub off on you, or a hero—who will help you navigate the stormy seas and achieve success?

*A Better Shot at Success*

In February 2014, Russell Wilson, quarterback for the Seattle Seahawks, led his team to its first Super Bowl win in the team's thirty-eight-year history. It was only Wilson's second season as a pro football player. At 5' 11" tall, he was not a likely quarterback. But Wilson had heroes who encouraged him, heroes who—through their noble actions—helped improve Wilson's lot in life. In an interview after the Seahawks' big win, Wilson talked about his parents, who saw his talent and the flame burning within: Russell's dream to become a pro football player. Through their noble actions, Mr. and Mrs. Wilson gave their son a better shot at success: They sent him to football camps and clinics, and constantly encouraged him. In a post-Super Bowl interview, Wilson talked about his dad: "My dad always asked me, 'Russ, why not you? Believe in yourself. Believe in the talent God has given you.'" As I mentioned, heroes come in all types of packages. Russell Wilson's heroes happen to be his parents.

## Attributes of Heroes

*Heroes are ordinary people who have achieved success.* My heroes are common, self-made men. They may have had very little material wealth growing up, but managed to figure things out and become successful. How? Probably by having heroes to learn from, and also by commitment to a vision, hard work, discipline, consistency, keeping their noses generally clean, understanding the importance of family and their God, serving and focusing on other people, and just showing up.

*Heroes are consistent. Their heroic acts aren't isolated incidents.* My heroes strove to fulfill the definition of a hero year after year. They were unwavering in their positive, pragmatic, successful patterns. Al Braca is a shining example of the consistency of heroes. On the morning of September 11, 2001, Jeannie Braca switched on the television to check the weather report only to hear that a plane had just hit the World Trade Center. Jeannie's husband, Al, worked as a corporate bond trader for Cantor Fitzgerald. His office was on the 105th floor of the North Tower. Al had survived the World Trade Center bombing in 1993 and had even helped a woman with asthma escape from the building. Jeannie knew that Al would do the same thing this time. She later said, "I knew he would stop to help and minister to people, but I never thought for a minute that he wouldn't be coming home!"

A week later, Al's body was found in the rubble. Then reports began to trickle in from friends and acquaintances. Some people on the 105th floor had made a last call or sent a final email to loved ones saying that a man was leading people in prayer. A few referred to Al by name.

Al's family learned that he had in fact been ministering to people during the attack. Rather than thinking of himself, he thought of others. When Al realized they were all trapped in the building and would not be able to escape, he shared the gospel with a group of fifty co-workers and led them in prayer to receive Christ. These were the very people who sarcastically nicknamed Al "The Rev." And yet, in the chaos of 9/11, he was the man they looked to—and he delivered.

The news came as no surprise to Al's wife. For years she and Al had been praying for the salvation of his co-workers. According to Jeannie,

Al hated his job and couldn't stand the environment because it was so contrary to his Christian values. But he wouldn't quit because he loved the people. Al was convinced that God wanted him to stay there to be a light in the darkness, and as it ended up—to be a hero.[1]

*Heroes are leaders.* Each of my heroes was a leader: they challenged me to be my best; they influenced me to do the right thing, and they seized opportunities to help me create results that otherwise may not have happened. In some cases, my heroes may have acted for the good of a team, but it was always for my good as well. Heroes almost automatically become leaders because others gravitate toward them, recognizing that they consistently exhibit patterns of noble acts, wisdom, and behavior. Others follow heroes, not only because heroes demonstrate success, but also because heroes work for the good of others and bring out the best in them.

*Heroes work hard, even when it isn't easy.* Heroes are not perfect; they are imperfect people who endeavor to do the right thing, even if sometimes they get it wrong. They get up the next morning and go right back at it, but this time a little differently, a little bit better—time and time again. *When they fail, heroes pick themselves and try again.*

*Heroes set noble goals.* Heroes aren't out for just themselves. In fact, it's the opposite. Heroes set goals that are generous, good-hearted, and well-meant. As they achieve these goals, they help others rather than themselves. *Heroes focus on others.* Missionaries David and Beth Grant did just that through a ministry called Project Rescue. The Grants began their work in India decades ago doing the usual missionary work of planting churches and building Bible colleges. It was in the late 1990s that God began to burden their hearts for the scores of women and children living in sexual slavery. The conviction that they could and should make a difference led David and Beth Grant to establish the ministry of Project Rescue. Since its inception, Project Rescue has ministered to over 32,000 women and children impacted by sexual slavery. Through aftercare homes, vocational training, after school programs, night care shelters, HIV/Aids and medical clinics, red light district churches and

---

[1]   http://www.sermoncentral.com/sermons/the-art-of-being-a-hero-kenneth-sauer-sermon-on-evangelism-the-lost-49978.asp

Sunday schools, and awareness and prevention programs, women and children are being rescued and restored.[2]

*Heroes set examples others can follow.* Heroes walk the talk, make mistakes, fall down, and get back up to save the day … time after time. They demonstrate long-term patterns of success by accomplishing pre-determined goals. Heroes teach us positive patterns of behavior we can emulate.

I can think of no better example of a man worth emulating than Jesus Christ. I've asked Rev. David Todd Weston to share how heroism is exemplified in Jesus, who demonstrated leadership and consistency, who focused on others and who set an example that is still being followed after two millennia:

> The childhood game "Follow the Leader" is harmless enough, even though the person designated as the leader might lead their followers through some interesting places. But in real life, following a leader can turn out to be a blessing or a curse, depending on the character and competence of the one leading.

In his book, *Developing The Leader Within You,* John Maxwell shared this leadership proverb, "He who thinketh he leadeth and hath no one following him is only taking a walk."[3] Jesus of Nazareth wasn't just taking a walk. He was a leader with a large following. The first century followers of Jesus Christ saw in him the attributes of the heroic.

His character was above reproach. It was Jesus who taught his followers to love their enemies, turn the other cheek, and go the second mile. Jesus' followers were fascinated with his teaching because he taught with authority that captured the heart. The authority of his teaching was based on his personal integrity. People believed him because they trusted him. Even Jesus' enemies who despised him could not make their accusations stick because his character was so thoroughly intact.

Like his character, Jesus' compassion was equally strong. Jesus was a leader who actually loved his followers and wanted the best for them.

---

[2]  Excerpt from article located at http://www.projectrescue.com/about-us/history

[3]  Maxwell, John, *Developing The Leader Within You,* Thomas Nelson Publishers, 1993, page1

Some modern-day heroes appear to care more about themselves than their followers. With Jesus it was just the opposite. He made it clear that he was more interested in serving others than in being served. Jesus demonstrated this sacrificial attitude by washing the feet of his disciples; a task reserved for servants. He then told his disciples to follow his example and do for others as he had done for them. Jesus was a hero who clearly demonstrated the life he wanted his followers to live by living it himself. And rather than modeling a condescending attitude, Jesus displayed an attitude of compassion.

The followers of Jesus Christ were also drawn to his courage. Here was a man who was not afraid to speak the truth, even though it ultimately cost him his life. Jesus lived in a world controlled by the powerful Roman Empire. Rome had a zero-tolerance policy toward anything that smacked of rebellion. To say the things Jesus said was dangerous indeed. But Jesus didn't say what he said or do what he did to pick a fight with Rome. He said what he said and did what he did because it was true and right. His followers have followed in his courageous footsteps from that day on and have changed the world.

Jesus was a hero worth following because his life commanded respect. Furthermore, he was one of the few heroes who actually loved his followers. He expected a lot, and he gave a lot in return.

OOO

Life is a series of challenges, filled with face plants and stormy seas. Heroes help us get up so we can continue forward and move toward success; they help us overcome the tests and trials we encounter as we go through life. When faced with tough times, we all need strength beyond ourselves; we all need something to hold on to so we can rise from the dirt and keep going. This is where heroes come in.

*Thank you to Pastor Todd Weston for his contributions to this chapter.*

## CHAPTER FIVE

# We All Need Heroes

Many young people are set up, often from the very beginning, to breed failure and not success. One element that contributes to this is *fatherlessness*. This single factor—just one component—has a staggering negative impact, and it's only one of many influences that breed failure rather than success in our society. There are many statistics on the impact of fatherlessness. Here are just three:

- 90% of homeless and runaway children are from fatherless homes.[4]
- 85% of children who exhibit behavior disorders come from fatherless homes.[5]
- 71% of high school dropouts come from fatherless homes.[6]

Many segments of the population do not have mothers, fathers, or anyone who has their best interests at heart. And when there is a parent, it's not always someone after whom we should model ourselves. The manifestation of *not* having heroes—from whom we can learn positive patterns and habits—are numerous: poor academic performance, prob-

---

[4] Source: US D.H.H.S., Bureau of the Census
[5] Source: Centers for Disease Control
[6] Source: National Principals Association Report on the State of High Schools

lems with family relations, substandard educational experiences, financial problems. Heroes teach us positive vision and values, patterns of hard work, honesty, consistency, and perseverance.

Our current educational system—with its dearth of experiential training—leads to many well-educated people with no life experiences or common sense. Without guidance, we don't always understand and recognize the positive patterns of behavior that lead to success, happiness, health, and wealth, nor do we know the empirical definition of success. So, instead of reaching for true success, today's youth often model their behavior after celebrities. This modeling and replication, more often than not, leads to negative outcomes.

Many of us choose a route of surrounding ourselves with friends or other influencers based on geographic proximity—next door, around the block, at school or church, in sports and clubs, at parties and in gangs. The importance of those with whom we surround ourselves cannot be overstated. Some (or many) of the characteristics these people possess will rub off on us: positive and negative, helpful and not helpful, characteristics that promote success—and those that don't.

When I make my list of heroes, my dad, though a good man, is not on the list. My mom was ill, very ill, and she is not on the list, either. My parents were not my heroes. (In fact, many people don't list their parents as heroes.) On the other hand, I have been fortunate to have six heroes, each of whom played a role in my success. When we have heroes, we are not alone. I often thought I was alone, but I wasn't. My heroes were there to help.

Whether we want to admit it or not, we need that help. Pastor Todd shares,

> A popular song says everyone needs someone to love. I would add that everybody needs someone to look up to. No matter who you are, we all need heroes. We need models to pattern our lives after because as the saying goes, so many things are better caught than taught.
>
> We all need heroes because none of us is born knowing how to do life. There's an often-repeated statement in the

Bible that applies to everyone, "I would not have you to be ignorant." Obviously, we all come into this world in that condition. The writer is simply telling us not to stay in that condition. Don't be a know-it-all. Realize you need help and that there are people all around you who can help. We all need heroes to instruct us, encourage us, and even correct us when necessary.

On our own, we're ill-equipped to face the challenges of life, or even to achieve success and happiness. Happiness is the single most sought after value that all human beings seek, yet, it's elusive—and, it's one of those values that "is better caught than taught." I believe that success by my definition (the achievement of a pre-determined, *noble* goal) leads to happiness. We know that we want to be happy, but many of us don't know how to get there. Unfortunately, it can take too many years of personal trial and error to ascertain the good and helpful patterns we need to use early and effectively. Heroes teach us methods and patterns of behavior that will support us in our quest for happiness, success, love, and achievement—in our eyes and others'.

**CHAPTER SIX**

# Tom Horton, My Safe Harbor

One of my happiest memories from my childhood is the weeks that turned into months that I spent with Tom and Dot Horton in Annapolis, Maryland. Mom and Dad were often feuding—and subsequently, living apart. When they were separated, Dad lived in an apartment near the Pentagon. Mom, my two brothers and I lived in our home in Chevy Chase, Maryland, just outside of Washington D.C.

Tom and Dot Horton knew me from the day I was born. Dot Horton and Aunt Jean were lifelong friends: They grew up one block away from each other in northwest Washington, D.C. Tom Horton was a cousin of Aunt Jean's husband, Uncle Chuck. A number of years after Tom and Dot married, they moved to Annapolis.

I believe Tom and Dot were never particularly fond of my father: I think they felt Mom and Dad were a bad match, and it was no secret that my parents were constantly quarreling. Tom and Dot provided opportunities for me to spend time with their family down on Chesapeake Bay, often for weeks at a time. Occasionally the rest of my family joined me, but more often than not, the Horton's home was my escape and I loved being there in a warm and loving environment. Tom and Dot had five kids; I was like their sixth. I thought then that I had to compete for attention, but as I look

27

back on it, I didn't have to compete very hard: I got plenty of attention from both Tom and Dot. I loved my time with them: I played all day with the Horton kids, and looked forward to the time Tom came home from work, with the hope that he would take me out in his sailboat. The Hortons had a dock in their backyard; their property was on a tributary going out to the bay. Tom had a nineteen-foot Marconi-rigged sloop, Lightning class. Learning to sail that Lightning was probably my first real goal, and Tom Horton helped me realize that goal. Two or three nights each week, Tom and I went out in this little sailboat on the Chesapeake Bay. He gave me his time, his patience, and experiential training in the fundamentals of sailing. I got pretty good at sailing, which became a lifelong passion of mine. Learning to sail was my true, first taste of success, and the experience taught me how to trust others. Sailing is still a passion of mine: I've owned a number of sailboats, most much larger than Tom's Lightning; I even became certified as a bareboat charter captain … all thanks to Tom.

Tom was vice-president of a technology company that produced acoustic sonobuoys for undersea submarine detection in warfare. On Saturdays, he often took me to his office with him, and let me "work" in the electrical shop; he showed me how to solder together transistors and circuit boards. I had no idea what I was doing—and certainly wasn't about to be hired by Apple Computers—but I felt as though I had learned something quite important because I was able to take the soldering iron and lead, and connect transistors to a circuit board. It was a great experience.

As a young man, Tom was an Olympic athlete in the sport of kayaking. When I visited the Hortons, I always had my eye on Tom's mahogany kayak hanging in the garage. I dreamed about being in that kayak. Tom promised me it would happen one day, and it did. It was a small kayak, and remember: I was a chubby kid. Of course I wanted to do an Eskimo roll. Doing so requires the utmost concentration along with physical ability—and good upper body strength—which I didn't have. I attempted my Eskimo roll, and flipped the kayak. There I was, hanging upside down in the Chesapeake Bay. Well, in the summer, the bay is infested with jellyfish. I was in only three feet of water, but within seconds, my face and arms were being stung. It was pretty ugly—but a fun experience all in all—and it taught me that it's okay to fail sometimes.

Tom also had a British Seagull, an old-style outboard engine. To get the motor started, you had to tie a rope around the top and spin it. Then the engine kicked over and you would be on your way. These engines are known for their reliance: They keep on ticking under almost any circumstances. Tom's British Seagull sat on a sawhorse in the garage. He commanded me more than once, "Never touch that when I'm not around." Well, Tom happened to also have a canoe with a flat stern—on which to put the outboard engine. I dreamed and schemed, probably for weeks, as to how I could secretly take the British Seagull engine, attach it to the green canoe that sat in the water next to the dock, and tool around the Chesapeake Bay.

One morning, Tom went off to work and Dot went shopping. I don't know where the Horton kids were. This was my chance! I quickly ran to the garage, unscrewed the British Seagull engine from the saw horse and carried it to the dock. While I attempted to secure the engine to the canoe's stern, the Seagull engine flipped off the stern, and sunk like an anchor into ten feet of water.

*Holy S\*\*\*!*

There I was, doing exactly what I was adamantly told not to do, and I ended up with the British Seagull Engine in water so murky that I couldn't see the bottom—or the engine. Instead of a dream come true, it was a nightmare. I ran as fast as I could to the garage, grabbed a rope, ran back to the dock and dove in the water, thrashing about looking for the engine. I could only see two feet in front of me and had to come up for air a couple of times. On the third try, I found it. I went up to the surface, took a big gulp of air, dove back down and tied the rope around the engine. Meanwhile, I was burned and stung again and again by legions of white jellyfish. I managed to pull the engine back on the dock; then, as quickly as I could, I maneuvered it back into the garage, and to its place on the sawhorse. My heart was beating furiously. *What if I broke it? What if it won't start?* I wrapped the rope around the engine and spun it. The Seagull coughed, sputtered—and then ran like a clock! *Phew.* I had done the very thing Tom—who was like a semi-god to me—told me not to do. I screwed up big time, and I paid the price emotionally and with more than a few jellyfish stings.

Now, the real question is, did I admit my sins to Tom when he came home from work? The  answer is no. In fact, I didn't admit a thing or even share the story with Tom until fifty years later.

OOO

Tom Horton was successful. He is Marine. (Once a Marine, always a Marine.) A true entrepreneur, he is internationally known and respected: A two-time Emmy Award winner, he worked with Jacques Cousteau and the Cousteau family, creating and producing *The Undersea World of Jacques Cousteau*. Tom also filmed many of the Discovery Channel's shark films, and filmed and produced the story of the Gossamer Albatross, a human-powered aircraft that crossed the English Channel in 1979.

Tom was married to the same woman for sixty-four years and had five kids. Neither accomplishment is an easy feat, but he managed to achieve both successfully, even if imperfectly. He is a Marine who is also warm and gentle. He showed me that not only should a man be strong and machismo, but he taught me by example that you need to have it all: You must be strong, rough and ready, and machismo, but you must also be sensitive, kind, warm, creative, constructive, good-hearted, good-spirited, and charitable. And, you must accomplish pre-determined goals.

I tasted success because of Tom Horton. I pointed my moral compass in the right direction because he taught me how to do so by his example. He is a man whom I respected and, in many ways, viewed with awe. He gave me a safe harbor, and some of the happiest times of my young life. He was—and is—positive, warm, creative, courageous, tenacious, focused, honest, noble, a man's man, an athlete, a Marine, a faithful husband and family man, and he's my hero.

## CHAPTER SEVEN

# Interview with a Hero
# Tom Horton

**When you consider Eric's concept of a hero, what comes to mind?**

*First of all, several words and phrases come to mind when I think about a hero: love, respect, hard work, success, pride, concern, support of family and friends, and not disappointing others. I hadn't thought of it this way, but those are actually all words I would use to describe Eric.*

*Typically we think of a hero as someone who commits an act of courage in the face of death, but for an "average hero," I believe it's someone who tries to help others—and that help can come in many forms. Heroes don't necessarily need to be asked for help and they aren't looking for payback. A hero steps up to the plate when he sees a problem because it's a natural thing for him to do. Most heroes don't know at the time that they are committing a heroic act.*

## Can you say a little more about heroes stepping up to the plate because it's a natural thing to do?

*Helping others is something you learn from those who help you. I first learned about helping others from my mother because she helped everyone around her ... my brother Mack and me in particular. Everything in the service—I was in the Marine Corps—is about taking care of and helping others, your fellow Marines. This whole business of helping others is a way of helping ourselves: There's a lot of self-satisfaction to be derived from seeing that others are happy or have achieved success because you reached out and helped them.*

## What has success looked like for you in your life?

*My biggest success in my own mind is that I was a good husband. If I've had other success in my life, it hasn't been the financial kind. It's been a wild ride: I've been on World War II aircraft carriers and submarines, and was involved in military electronics, mostly under sea, so I had a chance to dive 4,200 feet in a submersible. I was on two Olympic teams. I ran Jacques Cousteau's office in California for seven years. I raised over one million dollars for the human-powered airplane called Gossamer Albatross that flew across the English Channel on the power of the legs of the pilot—and then I got a contract to make a film about it, the first documentary I ever made. I produced over one hundred documentaries, including a two-hour special about John Kennedy for the 20th anniversary of the assassination. I've won two Emmy Awards. It's been a crazy ride and I thank God that every time I was in the jaws of disaster, I came up with some weird idea and saved our bacon.*

## Can you give an example of a time then a weird idea saved you from the jaws of disaster?

*After seven years with Cousteau, I landed a job with a small electronics company. I'd heard about a meteorological convention and got permission from my boss to attend. Dr. Paul MacCraedy, an aeronautical engineer, was attending the convention; I wanted to meet him, so I took him to lunch one day. I asked what he'd been up to and he pulled out a magazine with a picture of the Gossamer Condor, the first human-powered aircraft, on the cover. Paul had created the aircraft with a partner as an entry into the Kremer Prize competition; he and his partner won the prize money of fifty thousand British pounds (approximately eighty-three thousand dollars). The Kremer Prize organization then put up one hundred British pounds for the first human-powered airplane to cross the English Channel, twenty-six miles. But Paul didn't have the money to create this new aircraft. I signed a contract with Paul that I would raise the money and get ten percent of whatever I procured. As it turned out,* 🌿 *I obtained over one million dollars from DuPont, and Paul won the competition with his Gossamer Albatross.*

*Meanwhile, I'd lost my job with the electronics company and needed to find something to do: I was fifty years old and had five kids. An idea was born out of desperation and my imagination: I got DuPont to allow me to make a documentary about the Gossamer Albatross. I knew nothing about documentaries, but I'd had experience managing the Cousteau organization and dealt with writers, editors, and narrators. That first film won an Emmy and my film company was launched. That's how my wild imagination helped to save me and my family from the jaws of disaster. We ran that film company for twenty-eight years, and four of our five children worked in the business at various times. Eventually, we made the first shark film for the Discovery Channel, which started the "Discovery Shark Week," and then we completed thirty-three one-hour shark films over an eighteen-year period. But it's the two-hour special on JFK about which I'm most proud, and for which we won our second Emmy.*

**You've delved into and been successful at so many different things. To what do you attribute your success?**

*Four things: having a great sense of humor instead of a big ego, competitiveness, my imagination, and my wife.*

*I gained a wild sense of humor from my mother: She could take any disaster and turn it into a laugh. We didn't have much growing up: I had only one shirt and one sweater. Today, I've got more than one sweater, but that's not what's important. I've had a fun life. I look at myself and my life, and get a big kick out of it. If I screw something up, my ego never gets in the way. Instead of cursing, which I'm happy to do as a Marine, my sense of humor takes over and I just laugh at myself.*

*I think I became competitive without even knowing it, because I wanted to get a pat on the back. I wasn't a good student, but I was a good athlete. My father rarely had a good word to say about me; he didn't understand me and I didn't understand myself. I was probably seeking his approval. So much of who we are and what we achieve is a result of what we've learned from our parents. But, there is also some level of competitiveness in everyone who achieves—even if it's being competitive with oneself. You want to be a winner.*

*My wild imagination came from my dad. On Sunday mornings when we were growing up, my brother and I climbed into bed with our parents. Father had a colorful life, and told us stories about the things he'd done and the interesting people he'd met: He told us about growing up in northern Pennsylvania, his adventures in the woods, and raising a bear cub. He shared stories about the Spanish-American War, being a pilot in World War I, selling a car to a senator and helping to build the first airport in Washington D.C. My father could really spin a yarn, or "coax the birds out of the trees," as my mother used to say. I thought his stories were incredible. I tried to duplicate my father somewhat, and that's how I developed a wild imagination.*

*But behind it all was my wife Dot, who just kept patting me on the back and telling me it would all work out. She was always supportive. Whenever I wanted to change jobs, or do the next crazy thing, Dot had only one question, "Do you think it's the right thing for the family?"*

## Eric describes you as "the Marine who is also warm and gentle." Do you see yourself that way?

*I'm certainly not a fighter; I was never a fighter in my life. I went into the Marine Corps two months before I turned eighteen. I was really a little kid going off to Parris Island, and I didn't realize that if you go into the military, you're actually in competition. I did well in the military because I was very competitive and had been an athlete in high school. I guess you could say I'm warm and gentle, but I'm also very competitive and want to succeed.*

## Who in your life has been a hero?

*I've already mentioned my wife: She was my number one hero, always there, supporting me unconditionally. Dot and I knew each other seventy-one years, and were married just shy of sixty-four years.*

*There were two other heroes—people in my life who were always there for me: my older brother Mack, and a childhood friend. When my father died, I was fourteen and Mack was sixteen; Mack took me aside and said, "I'm your father now; you're going to do what mom tells you and if you don't I'm gonna knock the crap out of you." But he was always there for me. He told me we needed to work hard to help Mother. We got an old cow and some chickens: I milked the cow and Mack took care of the chickens.*

*Mack used to leave school in Silver Spring Maryland and drive to my school in Washington to take me to my track meet. He was always there rooting for me, and after the track meet, he bought me an ice cream cone. Now that I think about it, he too, helped me to develop a competitive nature by supporting me in my athletic endeavors. He went ballistic when I got into the Olympics, almost as though it was his victory, too. Mack was like a surrogate father: When I had a problem, I talked to Mack. He was worried about my grades and somehow arranged for me to go to high school in Washington D.C. I'm forever grateful to him for that; otherwise, I would never have met Dot. Mack was the student that I was not. He got straight As and was the president of his class; everyone liked him. He went to Yale as a Marine and was an officer when he graduated. He was proud of me because I quit high school and enlisted in the Marines. To the day he died, we always said, "I love you," before hanging up after a phone conversation.*

*My childhood friend, Jim, and I met in the fourth grade. I was always everyone's failure, but not his. In the 6th grade, Jim was a patrol leader and he raised the flag every morning. Jim told the principal he couldn't raise the flag by himself, and that he was going to ask me to help him. The principal asked, "Do you think he can?" and Jim replied, "Tom can do anything." I had a lot of people pat me on the back, and step up to the plate for me, but Dot, my brother, and Jim are my three biggest heroes.*

**Eric says he pointed his moral compass in the right direction because of your example. What principles have guided you throughout your life? Who or what has influenced you to live by those principles?**

*The first thing that comes to mind is that I was a good husband, and a good friend to all our kids. I always tried to do the right thing, and was dependable. But we go full circle again: My brother and I were in love with my mother; the three of us were a great team. My father didn't treat my mother well and my brother and I saw that; she didn't deserve it. Mother always instructed us to be polite, and to do the right thing. She had an enormous effect on both of us and my wife had that same effect on me. When I met Dot, I saw my mother. Two of my heroes helped me with my moral compass.*

**What drew you to Eric, and did you realize the impact you were having on him?**

*I was drawn to Eric because he was calm, he was polite, and he wanted to learn. And no, I never realized how much Eric appreciated our relationship. I am very proud to hear that I had such an impact on him, and I'm humbled. I never knew I was being a hero or a mentor; I'm forever grateful that I was able to help, and that he sees me that way.*

## CHAPTER EIGHT

# Richie Moran
# Walk the Talk

By the time I entered Manhasset High, I'd gone from the guy who was always the last one chosen to play pickup basketball and the last guy any girl wanted to kiss ... to not so bad. I was lean, mean, and ready. I'd had lots of experience making friends at a new school and within a week, found myself chumming around with a bunch of guys who played lacrosse. They knew I'd come from Maryland, another hotbed of lacrosse, and assumed I played. In spite of their surprise when I told them I knew nothing about the game, they told me that signups for lacrosse were the following week in the junior high school gymnasium, and that I had to be there.

My friends and I all showed up on the designated day to try out for junior varsity ninth grade lacrosse. As we sat on the bleachers, I heard a bellowing voice coming from the far corner of the gym. I looked over and saw the voice was that of a guy who was probably in his late twenties, ruddy complexion, short and stocky, and in great shape. He was loud and boisterous, and there was something about him—I'm not sure exactly what it was—that struck me from across the gym. He was talking with a bunch of coaches; that day was sign-up day not only for lacrosse, but for other sports as well, and each of these guys coached a different sport.

I continued to watch the animated conversations taking place at far side of the gym, when this guy, who seemed to be the leader of the other coaches, walked over to the bleachers. He stopped short, looked me right in the eye and asked my name.

"Eric Rieseberg," I replied.

"Have you ever played lacrosse?"

"No," I answered.

He picked up a defense stick, handed it to me and said, "You have now. And your name's not Eric. Your name is Enrique. My name is Richie Moran and I'm the high school varsity coach. You're going to start playing right now."

From that very first interaction with Richie Moran, I felt indelibly connected to him. He took me, a guy who had never even held a lacrosse stick in his hand, and led me to the point where I was occasionally playing varsity lacrosse as a ninth-grader. I certainly didn't play first string, but I played on the varsity team nonetheless—at a school that had heritage of producing some of the best lacrosse players in the world including Jimmy Brown, who is considered by many to be the greatest lacrosse player of all time.

Richie, a Marine, was a leader. He had the ability to lead—in particular, lead men-to-be—and through his leadership and coaching talent, get young men to strive for excellence and push themselves further than they ever would have without his guidance. After two seasons as my coach, Richie Moran left me—a tenth grader and rising lacrosse star—and Manhasset High School.

OOO

Richie was just starting his career when he coached lacrosse for Manhasset High. He left us to seize an opportunity and became the director of athletics at another high school on Long Island, where he started a lacrosse program. His career path eventually led him to become the lacrosse coach at Cornell University in Ithaca, New York, just across the valley from Ithaca College where I attended. I played lacrosse at Ithaca, and actually played against Richie and some of my Manhasset High School teammates who went to Cornell. (Those were the guys who had both the grades and the athletic prowess to get into Cornell, while I had to go elsewhere—more on that later.) I saw Richie Moran in 2013. It had been forty years since I'd seen him last. After the death of my wife, I'd been contemplating life, so to speak, and decided to take a road trip from southwest Florida, where I live, up the east coast. I'd heard Richie was still living in the town of Ithaca. I looked up his phone number and gave him a call.

He answered the phone, and I recognized his voice immediately. "Richie, this is Eric Rieseberg," I said.

"Eric Rieseberg. Holy smokes! I remember when we first met—I remember it like it was yesterday. Let's see … what number were you? Number fifty-seven, right?"

"Yes," I replied, somewhat shocked.

Barely taking a breath, Richie continued, "I remember the first day I met you in the junior high school gymnasium. You had never even picked up a lacrosse stick; I picked up that wooden defense stick, threw it in your arms and said 'You're going to start playing lacrosse for me.'"

In the forty years since I'd last seen Richie Moran, he had probably coached thousands of lacrosse players, and I knew he'd enjoyed a lot of success. Yet, he remembered *me*.

"Richie," I said. "I plan to be up in Ithaca. I'm going to visit my alma mater, Ithaca College, which I haven't visited since I graduated. I'd like to stop by."

"Oh, that's great. I want to introduce you to my wife. Why don't you just come spend the weekend?" he quickly replied. "Call me when you get into Ithaca."

I called Richie when I was about an hour outside of Ithaca. Richie's voice was enthusiastic, "Good, get yourself set up in your room, and then let's meet for drinks in the saloon at the yacht club at six o'clock. I'll see you there."

Richie Moran is a favorite son of Ithaca, New York. Being with him is like being with the president of the United States, perhaps. All evening long, there wasn't a single person who walked by our table without acknowledging Richie.

Richie stopped every one of them and said, "I want to introduce you to someone. This is Eric Rieseberg. He played for me at Manhasset High School and then played lacrosse at Ithaca College."

I was dumbfounded. This guy has coached and led national champions, college All-Americans, and American Hall of Fame guys. I'm nothing compared to them. But Richie Moran, forty years later, remembered everything about me: passes I missed, strengths I had, my uniform number, and the very day he and I met.

### OOO

The day Richie Moran left Manhasset High School was a sad day in my life. Richie Moran led me, challenged me, and energized me to go from never picking up a lacrosse stick to being pretty good. Consciously or subconsciously, I was looking for leadership, and I found it in Richie. I learned how to be authentic from the example set by Richie every single day: He walked the talk. When Richie was talking with you, he looked you straight in the eye— and he listened. He made you feel as though you were the most important human being in the world at that moment. He loved his players, and we all knew it. That's authenticity. Through his leadership and coaching, I learned that accomplishing a goal takes both hard work and perseverance: Richie put the team through an extraordinary amount of training. Even when it was snowing, we had to shovel snow off the parking lot so we could practice there. I learned that you do whatever is necessary to accomplish your goal. There's no question in my mind that if Richie Moran hadn't engaged me as he did that day in the gym, I would never have played lacrosse. Together, Richie and lacrosse gave me a new beginning, and became my only lifeline.

When Richie left, my world was destroyed: I was alone once again.

I realize now that while Richie wasn't physically in my life for forty years, he really never left. Richie is an exceptional man and an exceptional coach. He's warm, motivational, and disciplined—and he's my hero.

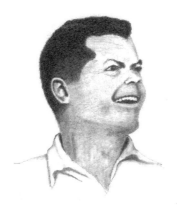

## CHAPTER NINE

# Interview with a Hero
# Richie Moran

**How do you define success, and on what do you base your own success?**

*Success is all about the joy I'm able to bring to another individual, and the joy I personally receive from helping someone become better and better. I've always been a caring and sharing kind of person, and that's the foundation from which I have always coached, and the foundation on which my success is based.*

*When it came to success, I always wanted to portray a good example for my players. I was concerned about young men sometimes putting too much effort into athletics, and not enough into academics. So I called my players to achieve the double AAs—*

*academics and athletics—and it worked out very well. If you're going to perform on the lacrosse field, if you're going to be a successful athlete, you can't have the weight of disappointment on your shoulders. That disappointment can be in the classroom or on the field.*

## Does money fit into your definition of success?

*Not really. Initially, I was interested in an industrial safety program, and was offered a job when I got out of the service. The position wasn't going to be available for four months, so I lived at home with my parents; I was single and probably overdoing it with my social life. One morning, my mother woke me up and said, "I think you're wasting your time. You have four months before you start a real job. Why don't you substitute teach in the meantime?" I always had great faith in my mother, so I got a substitute teaching job at my former high school—and never left teaching. My first substitute teaching job was working with disabled children; helping them improve their quality of life touched me deeply. Whenever I think things aren't going well for me, I reflect back to that class all those years ago and it really puts things in a proper perspective. Back to the money question: The job offer in industrial safety was for $27,000, and I took a $6,000 teaching job, so no, money wasn't a motivator for me and it's not part of my definition of success.*

## Who in your life has been a hero?

*My heroes were my parents, my family, and my high school and college coaches. My parents came to the United States as immigrants, seeking a better life. They taught their children never to take anything for granted, and set the foundation for me to be a caring and sharing person. My first recollection of truly sharing goes back to when I was six years old: We had a school project that involved sending letters to Boys Town, an organization that provides assistance to at-risk children. I remember sitting down with my parents and taping seventy-one cents to a card and sending it off to Boys Town with a letter. I've been contributing to Boys Town ever since. My parents taught me by their example to reach out and help others.*

*Bill Ritch, my high school coach—who is a Hall of Fame coach—really set the tone. Certainly he taught our team the value of discipline, but he also taught us the importance of respect for the program, our school, and our teammates. I also learned the importance of being charitable from him: As a team, we worked on community projects as well as projects at churches and synagogues. It was important for the community to realize we were more than just high school athletes.*

**Eric calls you "warm, motivational and disciplined." Who or what made you a disciplined person, and what role does discipline play in success?**

*I learned discipline first at home. We never sat down at the dinner table until my mother sat down. The youngest person at the dinner table always sat to the right of my father. Once we were all seated, it was incumbent upon someone to start a dinner conversation by asking someone else, "Tell us what was so important in your day today." Those family conversations taught me the art and discipline of truly listening to someone else. I was also taught by nuns in a parochial school, and that certainly helped me understand all about discipline.*

*The Marine Corps, of course, continued my education in discipline. I was in the Air Force ROTC at the University of Maryland, but withdrew from the program in my junior year because they increased the length of time grads would have to remain in the service. My withdrawal caused my draft status to immediately change to "eligible." I enrolled in the Marines and as a twenty-year-old, it gave me not only the discipline I needed, but I learned more about teamwork and love for others—in this case, love for my fellow Marines. The Marines helped me understand sacrifice. "Semper Fidelis" means always faithful. When you go into battle with a platoon of Marines, you may need to save the life of someone next to you. That's a lot of responsibility and there aren't any shortcuts. I've always told my athletes "You cannot take a shortcut to success. There will always be detours, bends, and caution signs in the road. Take the straighter way and believe in yourself and the principles taught to you by your parents and your family."*

**What drew you to Eric and what did you see as his greatest need?**

*I knew Eric was new to Manhasset, but had no idea about his athletic ability. I remember looking at him for the first time in the gym that day and we made great eye contact.*

*I said, "I know you're new to the area, and you're from Maryland, so you must have some idea what lacrosse is like."*

*He said, "Not really. Everyone here in Manhasset seems to be a lacrosse player, and I think I would be at a disadvantage."*

*"You'd only be at a disadvantage if you wanted to be. I want you to take this lacrosse stick and come back in a few days and let me know that you've made the decision you'd like to play lacrosse," was my reply.*

*Well, he came back in two days and from that point on it was a wonderful relationship. I was delighted that Eric got involved. He became a very fine player and carried his love for lacrosse into his life, including his business, friendships, marriage, and family. I think once he developed his skill for the game, he assumed a leadership role and became an outstanding teammate.*

*I always wanted to make a leader out of every one of my players: I had them lead calisthenics before practice, or take charge of a drill during practice. I asked them for comments during scrimmage time, and during games. Involving them made them feel more a part of the team; it made them feel like leaders—and those young men became ambassadors for the game of lacrosse. Leaders are ordinary people with extraordinary desire and I wanted to ensure that every one of my men who ever played for me could be a leader. I wanted them to be leaders, and I wanted them to be able to reach out and help others.*

**Eric talks about you coaching from love and being personally invested in the lives of others. How do those characteristics play a role in success?**

*I'm very humbled and honored to know that I've been able to assist others in any small way possible. I've mentioned Boys Town … their slogan is "He ain't heavy, Father, he's my brother," and their logo is a young man carrying his little brother on his back. I've been extremely fortunate to be able to carry a lot of people. I'm blessed to have been brought up in an ethnic neighborhood. Unfortunately, we no longer have that type of neighborhood. There wasn't a lot of wealth, but there was great togetherness and love for one another. We shared the grief and hardships—and we also shared the happy times. I loved it. To this day, I believe I was put in that neighborhood for a reason: It's part of what made me who I am.*

*One of the things I always wanted to do in life was to ask God if, for one day, I could cure all the young people in the world who have a disability; I think it goes back to when I taught that class of disabled children. I will always care. I will always share. I learned it from my parents. When I knew some of my players were having a tough time, whether it was at home, in a classroom, or on the athletic field, I always found time to be with them. Sometimes I took them to breakfast or lunch; I often had them come to my house and help me with something like raking leaves. One time I had three kids help me pull up a fence. Even now, when I see some of my players, we talk about those times. "Coach, how did you know that I really needed that?" they ask. "Well, I think the good Lord gave me the ability to recognize unusual situations in the lives of others," is my reply.*

*I end my conversation with all my former players and friends with "I love you." I say it because I mean it. When I spoke with Eric a few months ago, I think he was probably stunned that we hadn't spoken to each other in more than twenty years, and when we ended the conversation, I said, "Eric. Love ya."*

*I'm sure he got off that phone thinking "Wow. Why did he say that?"*

*Well … to me that's all part of success.*

## CHAPTER TEN

# Renzie Lamb and My Wakeup Call

During my sophomore year, I played second and third string on the varsity lacrosse team, though I sometimes sat on the bench. I thought the seniors were God's gift to the world; they were doing things in lacrosse that others only dreamed of. I guessed I was one of their heirs apparent—one of their great hopes—and I was feeling pretty good about myself.

We finished the season and I found myself not only being invited to all the beer parties with the seniors, but being kissed by a number of senior girls. I felt like a celebrity. Grades came out and once again, mine weren't very good; I still wasn't reading my textbooks or doing my assignments. At the end of the school year, I did my usual "summer thing:" I worked hard, giving sailing lessons and working on boats. I had also gotten into sports cars and fixing up Austin-Healeys.

The pressure to get good grades started to mount in junior year: college wasn't that far off and I had to get into a decent school. I took the college boards and did much better than my grades would have suggested. In fact, I did better than many students who had grades far superior to mine, but that wouldn't be enough to get into a good school. Meanwhile, things with my parents were getting worse. My mother was disappearing for a couple of months at a time, and then there was the incident when she tried to commit suicide.

And my hero, Richie Moran, was gone.

Our new varsity lacrosse coach was the former junior high school coach, Renzie Lamb; he was a great coach, esteemed by thousands of people … but not always by me. The chemistry wasn't always there. There was some arrogance on my part and it was probably obvious to Renzie. Most of the guys on the team grew up together playing lacrosse in their backyards; they'd all had sticks in their hands from the time they were eight years old. I'd held a stick for the first time just two years prior. I was popular: I had plenty of friends and did just fine on the dating scene, but the lacrosse guys were as thick as mud and I was the new guy—kind of an interloper. I recognized that, and planned to make my own name and my own way, with or without them. (Looking back, I realize that was a bit ridiculous since lacrosse is all about the *team*. Renzie probably thought I had a bit of a chip on my shoulder, which didn't help him as he was trying to build a cohesive team. In his "Marine Corps-style," he decided he would refine my behavior. At least that's what I thought.

The superstar seniors from last year's championship team had gone on to college, and Lamb had to build a team with players who were mostly just pretty good. We had two extraordinary players: Bob Rule, our goalie, was later inducted into the National Lacrosse Hall of Fame; Glen Mueller, an amazing player, was later inducted into the Cornell University Athletic Hall of Fame. The rest of us lacked this level of excellence, yet somehow, Renzie was able to galvanize a team of players who were not exceptional into a team that became national champions with a record of 18 and 0. And, many of my teammates became All-American players at elite colleges. To foster a national championship team with just two exceptional players was quite an accomplishment for Coach Lamb.

Renzie's style of coaching was quite different from that of Richie Moran: After one successful game when we were on our way to the 18 and 0 season, we were all feeling particularly proud—and probably a little bit cocky. Traveling back to Manhasset after winning 10-5, we were dead tired, sweaty, and sprawled out all over the bus. About five miles away from Manhasset High, Renzie stood up and told the bus driver to stop the bus.

"Get out ... every one of you!" he said. "Get out and jog the five miles back to the school. You won by only five points and you should have won by more."

That was Renzie. Relentless.

As a high school junior, I wasn't sensitive enough or smart enough to recognize that perhaps kindness comes in different packages: Renzie took me under his wing and invited me to his home for Sunday dinner a few times. With somewhere between twenty and thirty kids in the Manhasset lacrosse program, it was rare for a coach to be singling out a player and inviting that player to his home. On one of those Sunday afternoons, Renzie lost his temper with me. He started talking about my performance—or lack thereof—and started yelling and screaming at me, right at the dinner table. It seemed to come out of nowhere.

"You need to get your ass in line. I'm your coach, and you Manhasset guys, you may graduate, and in life you may be able to buy and sell me, but you'll never be a man," he bellowed at the top of his lungs.

Sometimes, the way we behave (as leaders, coaches, mentors) works, and sometimes it doesn't work so well. In Renzie's case at that moment, it didn't work so well: I dug in my heels and became a little bit more obstinate, a little bit more cavalier, and a little bit more sarcastic. I think that scene with Renzie Lamb screaming at me over Sunday dinner was the beginning of the end—and may have caused him to finally lower the ultimate boom on me.

In September of my senior year, I fell in love with a girl who attended St. Mary's, a nearby Catholic school. I took my girlfriend to her senior prom on a Friday night in early May. After the prom, we drank a few beers and celebrated. I got home at four in the morning, set the alarm for 6:45 so I could be on time for lacrosse practice, and fell into bed. Two hours later, the alarm went off as scheduled. I shut the off the alarm and rolled over. *I just need a few more minutes of sleep.* Those few minutes turned into a few hours, and I never made it to our Saturday practice. I let the team down in the final days of our championship run. I knew it then and it's even more evident to me now.

As I was suiting up for practice as usual on Monday afternoon, the team captain walked over to me and said, "The coach wants to see you."

"OK, I'll go see him as soon as I finish suiting up," I replied.

"No. He wants to see you right now."

"OK," I said, wondering what could be so important.

I made my way to Renzie Lamb's office and tapped on the door.

"You wanted to see me, Coach?" I asked.

Renzie stared at me for a moment and then mumbled something about my missing Saturday's practice.

"I overslept, I took my girlfriend ..." I started to explain.

"No explanation needed," he quickly interrupted. "You're off the team."

I couldn't believe what I was hearing. It was like my worst nightmare.

"Now get out of my office, go get your things, and get out of here."

One week later, my first real girlfriend dropped me for (in my mind) no apparent reason. For the next forty years, I had recurring nightmares about being kicked off the team. It remained deep within my mind as a total, embarrassing failure—something I would never let happen again!

In May of 1967, I lost the two most important things in my life: my place on a championship lacrosse team, and my first true love. More failure. More pain. More stormy seas. Meanwhile, my parents were separated. My mom's manic depression continued to worsen, and I had to involuntarily admit her to a psychiatric hospital more than once. New York State had gigantic, 2,000-bed mental hospitals. They were surrounded by huge brick walls; wrought-iron gates guarded the entrance. She was given electric shock treatments and was never the same person when she returned.

It was time for a change.

OOO

Renzie Lamb was and is successful. During our 18 and 0 championship season, he was also coaching football at Iona Prep, an all-boys Catholic high school in Westchester County, New York. He was named coach of the year in both sports as his teams turned in undefeated, untied seasons and won championships.

In 1968, opportunity knocked, and Renzie Lamb became the head men's lacrosse coach and the assistant football coach at Williams College in the Berkshire Mountains of Massachusetts. He produced thirty lacrosse All-Americans at Williams and retired with a 260-183-2 (.587) record.[7] The main playing field at Williams College is named after him.

When Renzie Lamb entered my life, I was focused on first on lacrosse, and then on girls, partying and sailing. I rarely picked up a book. Renzie taught me that I could be pushed and trained, and perform far beyond any limit I ever thought possible; that I could narrow my focus, concentrate, and achieve spectacular results. I learned from him that the team is more important than any individual—a concept that served me well in my career—and I learned the power of the combination of focus, discipline, and drive. Renzie Lamb is relentless, peppery, and acerbic, yet strategic and supportive. When I was seventeen years old, he gave me the biggest wakeup call of my young life. Renzie Lamb is my hero.

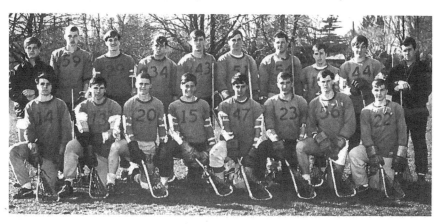

**VARSITY LACROSSE TEAM**
*Row 1, l to r:* M. Revello, J. Peterson, B. West, D. Fuchs, V. Martocci, G. Piccione, E. Rieseberg, P. Piccione. *Row 2:* J. Sicinski, G. Mueller S. Kaiser, B. Rule, J. Larmour, B. Ernst, T. Williams, T. Nicosia, P. Nowacek, Mr. R. Lamb (coach).

### 1967 Manhasset High School Championship Lacrosse Team (Eric Rieseberg #56)

---

[7] Source: www.Williams.edu

## CHAPTER ELEVEN

# Interview with a Hero
# Renzie Lamb

## What's a hero?

*A hero is defined by other people. I think back on my experience in the Marine Corps: heroes don't think about being heroes, and they don't necessarily think they are heroes. They just do the right thing. Eric's definition of a hero doesn't have anything to do with being in the service, but I do think there's a correlation in that Eric's heroes didn't set out to be heroes: They did the right thing; they did what needed to be done in the moment.*

## How do you define success, and what does your own success look like?

*Success is living a good life. By that I mean having discipline, integrity, and respect for others, and setting and achieving goals. Part of success is also how others view you. Your family loves you, and will stand by you unconditionally, but the way in which those outside the family think of you is a measure of your success. I think I've been successful: I've achieved what I wanted to achieve; I'm respected; I haven't cheated, lied or stolen. I've lived a good life. Money has never been part of my definition of success.*

## To what to you attribute your success?

*DISCIPLINE. If I had a tattoo, it would say "Discipline." And, if I had to attribute my success to only one thing, it would be discipline ... it's the cornerstone of a good life. The most challenging discipline experience for me was the five years I spent in the Marines, though it allowed me to truly understand the value of discipline, hone my management technique, and learn how to deal with men (through discipline).*

*There are two sides to discipline: one is self-discipline and adhering to set patterns of behavior, and on the other side of the coin is discipline imposed by others, and that involves not only adhering to certain patterns of behavior, but the correction of certain types of behavior. I had a lot of discipline growing up: My mother was a teacher and she ran the household—with my father's blessing. We never questioned anything my mother told us to do: we knew what we had to do, and we did it. I certainly had the correction type of discipline as well, both at home and school: I went to parochial schools and the nuns beat the s\*\*\* out of me, and later, I got thrown out of Catholic high school.*

*Loving what you do is another component of success. I always wanted to be a coach, and loved every day. Sure, problems come up, but at the end of the day, I was always able to look back and say to myself, "This was a good day," and I was always anxious to get out of bed in the morning. That's success.*

## How did you teach and model discipline as a coach?

*I think people—especially young people—crave discipline. It's like a warm coat: When you put it on, you feel safe and secure. I insisted on discipline when it came to team practice: we had a schedule and we were organized. I told my players what we were going to do, and we did it the same way every practice, no questions asked. They knew what to expect, so when they came on the field for their tenth or twelfth practice, they felt at ease and were able to focus. They were wearing the warm coat of discipline. I also tried to instill certain values in my players and I think that's part of discipline. First was respect. Other values I tried to instill in them were working hard, being prepared, and loving your teammates.*

## Did love play a role in your coaching?

*Absolutely. I loved my players—a coach has to love his players. They voluntarily come to you and want to play your sport. It's always interesting to outsiders: You kick the players' asses around, make them run home from games (even though they won), and the outsider asks the players, "Why do you love this guy?" It's because I loved them and they knew it. If anyone ever criticized a member of my team, I would be at their throat. The saddest day for the team is the last day of team practice. The group is ending. I never go to graduations because I hate goodbyes. These players are my friends, I love them, and they're not coming back. As a coach, you have to love your team. It doesn't matter if they love you back.*

*That brings to mind another incident: Eric described one day when the team won by five points; yet, you stopped the bus and made them run five miles back to the school because they didn't win by a big enough margin.*

*I remember that. The coach from the other team was a college friend of mine and I knew that my Manhasset team had the ability to destroy this other team, which didn't come close to Manhasset in terms of ability. I didn't want my team to be intimidated by any other team's circumstances, but in this case they were: they were intimidated by their opponent's lack of ability, and they played only well enough to win. It wasn't fair to the other team who expected more from Manhasset. I was not only displeased, but I was embarrassed. If you're good, then be good. Where was the effort? Manhasset didn't show the effort and therefore demeaned the opponent. Making them run back to the school— and I don't think it was five miles—is another example of giving them toughness.*

## Is there someone in your life you consider a hero?

*My mother. Before we had this discussion, I always thought of heroes as military heroes. But now, I realize my mother was a hero to me. Eric's concept of a hero has to do with improving and influencing the lives of others; that idea has grown on me, and that's exactly what my mother did. She was a unique person: a well-respected teacher, and one of the first women in New York to get her Master of Marine Biology. When I was thinking about going into teaching, she said, "Renzie, don't ever believe the saying 'If you can't do, then teach.'" She also told me she'd never met a man in education whom she could respect. Both of those things she said had a significant influence on me and my success.*

*My mother had a lot of self-discipline … she had to in order to take care of the family and the house, and do her job. My father was ill for many years and my mother took care of him. She never looked for praise, she never complained. And, she instilled disci-*

*pline in her children. We never questioned her. When I talk with my daughters, it's also evident that my mother was very influential with them, especially in terms of integrity.*

*My mother really was a hero, and I'm very happy to think of her that way.*

**Eric remembers a time when you had him to your home for Sunday dinner, during which you had some strong words for him. Do you recall that incident?**

*I always tried to get the seniors over to the house for dinner. At Williams College, I would notice that one player in particular seemed to need a little TLC, a little touch of home life. At Manhasset, it was simply an opportunity to thank them and learn about their future plans. That's not something we ever had time to talk about during practice or a game. In both cases, it singled out the individual and made them feel important. I can remember as a player being invited over to the coach's house and feeling very special. It's not special, but in the eyes of the beholder, it is. I don't recall the exact circumstances around the situation with Eric on that Sunday, but the way he tells it sounds like me (although he may have embellished it a little bit). Those Sundays were also an opportunity for me to motivate my players, and if I wasn't pleased with them, to let them know.*

*Here's an interesting thing about my career: at Iona Prep, Manhasset and Williams, the kids were privileged. They generally came from good families who were financially successful, and these kids had pretty much everything. I had to figure out a hook. What did they want, and what did they need? The one thing I discovered they didn't have was toughness, both emotional and physical toughness—and that's what I was able to offer them. I taught them to work hard, run hard, stand your ground, and how it translated off the field. When needed, I didn't hesitate to give them some tough love. That's what I was doing with Eric that day.*

**Eric says that being thrown off your team was life-changing for him. Did you ever wonder if you did the right thing by throwing him off the team?**

*I was twenty-seven when I threw Eric off the team. I'm seventy-seven now. For fifty years, there was always a constant question in my mind: Did I do the right thing?*

*Eric was above average when it came to lacrosse, a big contributor. He was well-liked and a good team player who never complained. I saw future potential for him and thought his better days for lacrosse would be in college. However, we had rules* and *"never miss practice"* was one of them. On the Friday night before the Saturday morning practice, Eric came up to me and told me he was going to St. Mary's prom that night. I said, *"Great. Have a good time. Just be at practice tomorrow morning."* And then he didn't show up.

Throwing Eric off the team wasn't an easy decision from a team perspective because I didn't have a lot of kids on the team and Eric was a contributor. But, my decision had to be based on rules and discipline—nothing else. Eric had let his team down.

I certainly didn't do it to make Eric's life miserable. My philosophy has always been that there's a bell curve on a lacrosse team: there are ten kids on the team. Two love you as the coach, two hate you, and six don't care. When I threw Eric off the team, he went from one end of the bell curve to the other. I always worried that he didn't take too kindly to what I did. Occasionally, we had a player who wasted his life. I never heard anything from Eric or about him. I worried how his life went. Also, I don't want to pass away with a lot of people thinking I'm a s***head.

**Eric says he learned the importance of a team because of you. Do you think that valuing the team above the individual is important to achieving success?**

Absolutely. It's everything. There is no "I" in team. When you're part of a team, you're playing for everyone on the team—so they are successful, and together you all are successful. When Eric made a decision not to come to practice, he hurt not only me, but his teammates. He let them down. That's the value of team: to be part of a group and to have the group be part of you.

**Did you have any idea you've had such an influence on Eric?**

No idea. People come to me and say *"You changed my life,"* and now Eric is saying the same thing. I certainly don't think of myself as a hero, but I accept that designation. You never know: One little remark or one action on the part of a leader can change a person's life. It's a legacy that must be held dear. As coaches, we have such an influence on these kids—it's a tremendous responsibility.

After throwing Eric off the team, it was fifty years before I saw him again. We had a reunion at Manhasset High School, and at that reunion, Eric came up to me and thanked me for what I did for him. That's the kind of reward you get in teaching and coaching—someone telling you that you changed their life. I've never consciously tried to change someone's life. I was just being me.

## CHAPTER TWELVE

# Stormy Seas

I graduated from Manhasset High School in May of 1967. Upon my graduation, my mother gave me an extraordinary gift: a personal letter from a mother to her son. Writing letters was customary for Mom. She was especially articulate, and had the most beautiful handwriting. She always wrote in a delicate script using her Tiffany fountain pen with indigo blue ink, on pale blue onionskin paper. When a letter was finished, she gently folded it, placed it in its matching blue envelope, and carefully sealed the envelope by dripping wax on the back. She then took a small bronze stamp etched with her coat of arms, and pressed the stamp into the hot wax. I'd watched my mother write letters and seal her envelopes since I was a young child, but this was the first time she had written a letter to me. Knowing that I loved to sail, Mom used sailing as a metaphor: She wrote about my embarking on a voyage, now that I had graduated from high school and said, "We all hope for calm waters. My wish for you, however, is that you come up against the occasional stormy sea to test your mettle and build your character." I've scoured my files and boxes of keepsakes a dozen times in search of that blue onionskin envelope—to no avail. I wish I still had it.

My mother got her wish. I can't say I've had a rougher life than anyone else—I certainly don't see myself as a victim—but I've had my share of challenges. Some storms are longer and more outrageous than others, but then, the storm goes away and the seas become calm again. In an odd way, I've enjoyed many of my life's stormy seas, and realize that my time spent at the helm of a sailboat has been a metaphor for the way I've lived my life: The winds and the seas of a squall combined with the heightened humidity and smell of seaweed has always provided a psychological comfort in an environment of pending danger. The fear of failure propels me: Given my years of sailing experience, I have the ability to competently and confidently captain any size sailing ship through a powerful gale ... with just a hint of apprehension based on the small possibility of failure. And so it is with my life: That constant fear of failure, the thinking that I can never be good enough, is a perpetual theme in my life.

Many of my classmates—especially my lacrosse teammates—deservedly went on to Ivy League and other top-notch schools. I'd realized too late the importance of buckling down academically and ended up going to the University of South Carolina. I didn't exactly buckle down there either, and my first semester was disastrous: I got a C, a D, and two Fs. The highlight of every week was that my biology lab partner was Miss South Carolina: I got to dissect a frog—with my forehead to hers—every Saturday morning.

When second semester rolled around, the one thing that was top of mind for me—and every freshman—was spring break. Fort Lauderdale was where everyone planned to go, but a buddy and I decided we didn't want to go anyplace conventional; we wanted to go to the Bahamas. We figured we could drive my buddy's car to Miami and then take a puddle jumper to Nassau in the Bahamas, but ... it would cost money, and Dad had continued to prudently control the amount of money I was getting. So, I called him.

"Hi Dad," I greeted him cheerily when I heard his voice on the phone. "I'm calling to get an advance on my allowance. A buddy and I are going to the Bahamas for spring break,"

"You're not going on spring break," he said with authority and some anger. "You're going to stay in the dorms and study."

I wasn't about to be denied what I thought of as a rite of passage. However, I didn't think fast enough before replying. The dorms are closed during spring break, but instead of telling him that, I replied with an arrogant "I'm going anyway."

"Where will you get the money?" was his next question.

"I'll just sell my books!" I answered.

I don't recall my dad's exact response, but he basically went through the roof—and I sold my books, went off to the Bahamas, and had a great time.

A couple weeks after spring break, I was sitting on the steps of the South Carolina capitol building, listening to the radio with my girlfriend. Otis Redding was singing *Sittin' on the Dock on the Bay*; an indescribable feeling washed over me when I heard the words "wastin' time." That feeling was fear. Fear of failure. *That's exactly what I've been doing!* I was all but flunking out of school. *Maybe I'm not as smart as I thought I was.* I had experienced fear of failure before, but never so poignantly. *The rehearsal is over*, I thought to myself.

At the end of the second semester of my first year in college, I went back to Long Island, tail between my legs, but with a new attitude—even though my dad delighted in telling me, "I told you so." I registered at Nassau Community College because I figured out that if I went to summer school, I could matriculate. Any grade below a C would be dropped and if I did well in summer school, by the fall I'd be fully enrolled at Nassau Community with a C or above. I went to summer school and for the first time in my life, I paid attention in class and completed my assignments. I finally opened the books—and tasted something new: academic success. I'd finally begun to find my sea legs.

In spite of dealing with more than my share of pain and failure, I was blessed with a number of positive influences, including my three (so far) heroes. And, that summer, I met Carolyn, the love of my life. Carolyn provided a safe harbor and had a positive, stabilizing influence on me. I began to excel in academics and earned very good grades at Nassau Community. I applied to other schools, including the NYU Stern School of Business and Ithaca College (just in case). I was accepted at Sterns and very excited about it. The very same week I was to pick up the keys to my dorm room at Sterns, I received a call from Ithaca College. They told me about their new hospital administration program and said they thought I'd be a good candidate for it. I went up to Ithaca and began to get very excited about the idea of hospital administration. I said thanks but no thanks to Sterns and transferred to Ithaca.

They happened to have a lacrosse team at Ithaca, so that was a plus. Halfway through the season, though, I had another epiphany: Lacrosse just didn't give me the thrill it once did. The sport had lost its place as one of the most important priorities in my life. I'd played for the best lacrosse coaches, and now I was playing for a Division III NCAA school, team, and coach. (To put things in perspective, in the late 1960s, the Manhasset High School team could beat a college Division III school's team. When Ithaca played Cornell in a scrimmage, we were crushed.) I quickly found the leadership was very different from the type that Richie Moran and Renzie Lamb had provided, and decided to quit the team to focus on my studies in hospital administration. A few months before graduation, I began applying to graduate schools. There never seemed to be any doubt I would go to graduate school, but although I was finally doing well, school wasn't where it was at for me. I wanted reality—not academics.

I graduated from Ithaca in January of 1972 and accepted an interim management position at North Shore University Hospital in Manhasset, with the understanding I'd leave for graduate school in summer or fall. I had applied to eight grad schools and got into seven of them, although I still didn't make the Ivy League: Yale didn't accept me. I decided to go to the University of Pittsburgh School of Public Health, and Carolyn and I married during my first year there. I also found myself falling in love with hospital administration in the same way I'd fallen in love with lacrosse, so when I received my master's degree, I set a very high goal for myself—to become a hospital administrator by the time I turned thirty. I would achieve that goal four years early.

My first job after grad school was as administrative assistant for planning and implementation of new services at Mercy Hospital in Denver, Colorado. It didn't take me long to realize that my boss wasn't someone I wanted to hook my wagon to: He didn't lead me, and he didn't light my fire. I worked for him for two and a half years while plotting my resignation. Then I was offered a position as assistant administrator at a hospital back east, Garden State Community Hospital, a brand new, 204-bed facility. I worked for a great guy who motivated me in the same way I'd been motivated by Richie Moran and Renzie Lamb. I loved my work; I showed up early and stayed late. I worked nights and weekends. *Harder, faster, stronger,* better became my mantra. We became the highest performing hospital in a company of fifty hospitals. Two years into my tenure with Garden State Community Hospital, my boss announced his resignation—and I became CEO at age twenty-six. I'd proven myself and was fortunate the board of directors had enough faith in me to think I could pull it off. Everyone in the entire hospital would be working under my leadership; I was the youngest of the team by far, but the boss.

It was only eight years earlier that Mrs. Crane, my high school guidance counselor, had told my parents I should become a welder.

Mom and Dad had finally divorced in 1972—when I was graduating from Ithaca, engaged to be married, and focusing on the future. Mom had gotten herself back on her feet. Her alcoholism was under control, and she was taking lithium for her manic depression. She started dating. Things got better and better. And then, one year into my appointment as CEO at the hospital, I received a phone call at two o'clock in the morning: Mom had choked to death in a restaurant. She was fifty-four years old.

After three years at the helm, Garden State Community Hospital was bought out by a large healthcare conglomerate, and the culture changed dramatically. The number one focus of the new management was money, but it wasn't mine. I never cared that much about the smell of money because cash wasn't what motivated me. I just wanted to work my hardest and be the best at what I was doing. So I put my résumé out on the street again and accepted a position as administrator of the largest hospital in the Tenet Healthcare Corporation. Life was good, and I had every reason to be happy. Not only had I met my career goal of becoming CEO of a hospital by the time I was thirty, but I had two CEO positions by that age.

Another high point was the adoption of our daughter, Kimberly, though her early life got off to a rocky start: She was born prematurely and had to be transferred to a neonatal intensive care unit at a hospital more than a half hour away. Kimberly spent over a month at that hospital, and Carolyn was there every single evening, feeding Kimberly with a syringe. I began to feel the true taste of success, that pot of gold at the end of the rainbow many of us were brought up wanting to achieve: I had a great job, financial security, and a beautiful family.

But then my world came crashing down, and I realized that bigger isn't always better. Issues of honesty and ethics started to bubble up in my life. Being highly paid and recognized led to seduction attempts by others, and this was disheartening to me. I wasn't brought up that way. I quickly learned some others were made of a different fabric, a different weave, and I was uncomfortable. Within two weeks of becoming CEO of this hospital, I had my résumé out on the street again. I decided I wanted to go back to a non-profit hospital, and this time I would be extremely selective. Before long, I was offered a CEO position at a small non-profit hospital in Vermont, and I took it.

When Kimberly was two and a half, we moved to the land of sleigh bells, snowshoes, maple syrup, and wonderful people. On the first day in my new position, I was able to review the revised hospital financial books. I learned several problems existed that I hadn't been made aware of—specifically, there was an attempted unionization and the hospital was about to go belly up. I was faced with trying to turn it around. Once again, I found myself working nights and weekends, but this time was different: I had the dedication, but not the enthusiasm. I had no heroes in my life to whom I could turn; the idea of idyllic Vermont went out the window. And then, our daughter was diagnosed with brain cancer.

We'd been in Vermont for eighteen months when Kimberly was diagnosed with a malignant brain tumor. She was treated at a nearby hospital, one of the best in the country, and the cancer went into remission. Twelve months later, the cancer returned and Kimberly was hospitalized again. Kimberly became quite a celebrity on the pediatric unit during her stay. On February 1st, for some reason she started giving away her toys and other childhood belongings to the other children on the ward.

On February 3rd, Kimberly was rushed to the ICU with an extraordinarily high heart rate, and her heart subsequently stopped. She was defibrillated a number of times to no avail. I held Carolyn in my arms while we hovered in the waiting room, anxious for word from a doctor. Finally, a physician appeared.

"Your daughter's heart has stopped. Do you give us permission to defibrillate again?" he asked quickly.

"Yes," we replied in unison.

Kimberly was resuscitated, but her heart stopped again. It was time to tell the doctor, "Do not resuscitate." I can still feel Carolyn's hands gripping my shoulders after we uttered those words and collapsed into each other's arms. At age three, one day before her fourth birthday, our precious Kimberly died. It was the most difficult thing I'd ever gone through. I was a parent, and I was supposed to protect my kid. But I couldn't; it was out of my control. I thought I'd seen the pot of gold at the end of the rainbow—and then my daughter died.

## CHAPTER THIRTEEN

# Bill Kaplan
# The Importance of Vision

There had been one bright spot in our Vermont sojourn: the adoption of our daughter, Jennifer. She was born in my hospital, and we adopted her two months after Kimberly was diagnosed with brain cancer. Ultimately, Carolyn and I decided to leave Vermont: We feared we'd always be known by the locals as "poor Mr. and Mrs. Rieseberg, whose daughter died when she was only four years old." I started looking for another job.

After Kimberly's death, the familiar feeling of fear was ever-present. Perhaps it was fear of death—or maybe even fear of life—but whatever it was, I decided to fight it off by toughening my physical and emotional self. I trained for and ran marathons, and participated in several experiential training programs including mountain climbing and living on an island for days with just the clothes on my back and a gallon of water. Failure had become more than a possibility—it had become a crushing reality, and fear of experiencing it again drove me to experiences in which it could be overcome. Somehow, I believed that pushing myself to the brink, via my participation in these outdoor expeditions, would protect me and my family from death, disease and disaster.

How wrong that would ultimately prove to be.

During one of these programs, participants were instructed to envision their desired future, and then to write a letter to themselves and their families, describing the future they hoped for. I wrote a five-page letter addressed to Carolyn and Jennifer, clearly outlining what I wanted to accomplish in the coming years. One part of my vision was that I would retire in fifteen years, at age fifty. This part of the letter was quite detailed, down to the place we would retire, and even a description of the house we would live in. When I returned home, Carolyn and I read the letter together, then put it in a chest and forgot about it.

A couple of months into my job search, I had the opportunity to interview at St Luke's Hospital—one of the roughest, toughest hospitals in the country—in a bad Newburgh, New York neighborhood. It was a 300-bed hospital, one of the least profitable in New York State. It was a disaster: Not only was the hospital hemorrhaging money, but the board of directors had just fired their tenth CEO in ten years. St. Luke's had hired Hospital Corporation of America (HCA), the world's largest hospital management company; they hadn't succeeded in fixing it on their own because it was such as mess. I kind of liked what I saw; I didn't recognize it at the time, but I needed a big challenge in which to bury my grief. I needed success again: I had failed my child. I saw my daughter's death as my own personal failure. I was a hospital expert, yet, I couldn't save her. I needed a mountain to climb, and I needed success.

I interviewed with the entire board, a bunch of stoic, street-smart, older guys. They were a formidable group, mostly hard-nosed, successful business people with "take no prisoners" attitudes. As individuals and as a group, they had a vested interest—emotionally and culturally —in ensuring the hospital got back on its feet.

"You can't do this. You're too young," said the vice-president, as he looked over to Bill Kaplan, the chairman.

I looked the vice-president square in the eye. "The hell I can't. I've done it three times already," I replied.

I looked over at Bill Kaplan and saw a big grin on his face.

"You're the guy," said Bill.

I knew I could—and would—do the job. I didn't like failure. I feared it, and it was the last thing I wanted to taste again.

I signed a three-and-a-half-year commitment with HCA, with the understanding that I was brought in to turn the hospital around. Within two weeks of my arrival at St. Luke's, it became very clear to me that there were far more problems than just those about which the board was aware. I discovered an issue with the anaesthesia machines in the operating room: They hadn't been properly maintained—undoubtedly for lack of funds—and patients' lives were being put in jeopardy. And there I was, this new, young, upstart CEO, with a big decision to make: I could sweep it under the table, I could subtly fix one or two machines, or I could go full bore and draw the line. It was an easy decision: I called an emergency meeting of the board.

"Ladies and gentlemen, we have a serious problem, and it needs to be addressed at once—right here, right now," I began.

After explaining the problem, I continued, "There are two options: We can find the money to replace these machines. Or, we can close down the operating room immediately."

The board members were shocked. Closing down the operating room of a hospital is a difficult, detrimental action—the equivalent of cutting your jugular vein, since the OR is the lifeblood of a hospital. Initially, the board pushed back and asked a lot of questions. No one ever said it, but I'm sure some of the board members were thinking, *who does this guy think he is? He's been here only two weeks, and he calls an emergency meeting to tell us we might need to shut down the operating room.* An emotional discussion ensued.

Within a half-hour, Bill Kaplan said, "We'll find the money. Get the new machines."

He had led the board to make the right decision for the patients, and the hospital. No doubt, Bill Kaplan faced disbelief from the board members about the state of affairs of the operating room. They probably asked him if this new, upstart, too-young CEO was telling the truth—or just causing a lot of drama. Bill Kaplan was always willing to stand up for what's right and best, no matter the circumstances.

Approaching the board with a major problem just weeks after my arrival tested my mettle: It could have been a career-limiting move, but it was my only choice. Looking back on my career, the board of directors of St. Luke's Hospital was, on one hand, the toughest board I've ever worked with: They tested me early, and they tested me hard. On the other hand, they were the easiest: In three and a half years, I had close to forty meetings with the board and they never once rejected any proposal I made. Our teamwork was remarkable and I give Bill Kaplan credit for consistently galvanizing the board—better than any board chair I have ever worked with. Even if the hill is steep and you need to take the hard road, if Bill Kaplan believes in the mission, it will get done.

St. Luke's had more than just equipment problems: They had quality of care problems, physician problems, and labor problems. When I arrived at that hospital, I had no intention of accepting anything but success: I'd had my taste of success in life—and I'd had my taste of failure. I knew the difference and wasn't about to eat dirt anymore. I'd just lost my daughter; I felt I'd had about all the character-building experiences I needed to last my entire life. What I needed was to taste victory again, and our team accomplished a fantastic turnaround at St. Luke's. We first addressed the immediate problems, and later opened a multi-modality breast imaging and health center for women. In addition, we opened new parking areas and added new state-of-the-art ICU equipment.

We also opened the first Medicare-certified hospice in the country, in Newburgh, New York, sixty miles north of New York City. It was Bill Kaplan's idea, and he put tremendous pressure on me as the CEO to start this hospice.

"'I can't do that; it's never been done. There are federal regulations, and it would be a pain in the neck," I said to Bill.

"You've got to do it. *We've* got to do it," was Bill's simple reply.

Bill started a foundation with his own money to get the hospice going. It was a nightmare to get a hospice approved in New York State, but we did it.

At the end of my tenure with St. Luke's, the hospital had gone from losing millions and risking insolvency to turning a profit.

I couldn't have become successful at St. Luke's without the help of Bill Kaplan. A stereotypical New Yorker who came from an entrepreneurial family in Brooklyn, Bill started a small manufacturing company in a crumbling warehouse about a mile down the road from St. Luke's Hospital—and eventually became a supplier to a major retailer. Bill was both charitable and noble in his undertakings, and took on very tough endeavours like the chairmanship of St Luke's Hospital. He did it because he's all about helping others.

I left St. Luke's at the end of my contract and talked with Bill Kaplan only twice in the next twenty years. Once he called me to ask me to come back to St. Luke's. The conversation didn't get very far when I told Bill how much he'd have to pay me. And then, twenty years after I'd left St. Luke's, he called again.

"Eric, it's been a long time," he began. "How are you?"

I was a bit perplexed as to why he would be calling me.

"Eric, you know that hospice you started? Well, we now have a new hospice building; it's just like a hospital. We're planning a fund-raising celebration, and we want you to come. You made this happen," he said.

That wasn't true. Bill Kaplan made it happen, and I *helped* make it happen.

"Bill, it's great of you to think of me, but I don't see Carolyn and me getting on an airplane and flying from Camden, Maine down to Newburgh, New York." I answered.

But he wouldn't take no for an answer. Bill and Dick Drake, the board VP, flew us down and Bill Kaplan himself picked us up at the airport and drove us to the hospice, where hundreds of people were ready to celebrate its opening. There were twenty or so people gathered together in the middle of the room. I noticed Dick Drake, who was vice-chair when I was at St. Luke's, so Carolyn and I walked over to say hello.

Dick looked at me and then addressed the group, "Excuse me everyone. I want to introduce you to Eric and Carolyn Rieseberg. Some of you were with St. Luke's when Eric was CEO. He was—and is—the best CEO St Luke's has ever had."

A mix of emotions ran through me. Dick rarely said much about anything or anyone, yet there he was, telling a bunch of people that I was the best CEO they'd ever had. There weren't many times in my life that I felt so much emotion over my accomplishments. In fact, it would be another twenty years before I had those feelings again.

Bill Kaplan is happiest when he's serving others. He was—and is—an entrepreneur, a visionary and a philanthropist. After I left St. Luke's, Bill went on to found A.C. Moore, an arts and crafts retail chain that has grown to 135 locations today.

On that same road trip during which I saw Richie Moran, I also stopped to see Bill. We met for lunch and I was bubbling over after my time with Richie. I could see Bill's wheels turning and asked what he was thinking.

"I don't want you to say another word," he said. "We're going to have lunch, and then I'm going to show you something."

After lunch, Bill took me to the Newburgh Armory, an old military armory. He opened the gigantic doors and then flicked on the arc lamps. Suddenly, the whole place was lit up like a stadium: right before me was a lacrosse field, complete with two lacrosse cages and brand new, never-been-played-on artificial turf.

"You're going to help me," Bill said. "I'm focused on teaching underprivileged kids how to read. I'm starting a reading program right here at this armory, and as an incentive to these kids, once they complete the three-month program and learn how to read, they can learn to play lacrosse. You know better than I, Eric, that if you get good grades in high school, and can play lacrosse, you can go to a hoity-toity school with a scholarship. You can go to Williams, Cornell, Yale, or Harvard. We can get these underprivileged kids into Ivy League schools."

"Okay Bill, what do you want me to do?" I asked.

"I want you to call Richie Moran, and get him to help me. I want a lacrosse program started down here. I'll fund it."

"Okay," I said, understanding what Bill had been pondering when I was talking so passionately about Richie, someone Bill had never met, over lunch.

"When?" he asked.

"Right now," I answered while grabbing my cell phone, and dialled Richie's number.

Richie answered right away. "Is everything alright? You just left here!"

"I'm with Bill Kaplan. He wants your help in starting a lacrosse program for underprivileged kids down here in Newburgh," I said.

"When does he want me?"

"Next week," I answered.

"I'll be there," was his reply—no questions asked.

So, Bill Kaplan and Richie Moran continue in their roles as heroes: They are working together to accomplish noble goals to improve the lives of others.

I have no doubt the lacrosse program will be a success. Bill Kaplan is abrupt and tenacious, and once he starts something, he doesn't stop until it's finished. We did a lot of innovative things at St. Luke's, but none of them would have happened without Bill Kaplan: I had my plate filled with day-to-day issues and early on I had neither the vision nor the desire to think about things like a hospice or a women's health center. They were Bill's ideas, and he taught me the importance of having a vision. Bill Kaplan allowed me to take bold steps at St. Luke's when many board chairmen would have just folded their tents. He had faith in me, he taught me, and he supported me to do the right things to turn St. Luke's around; ultimately, those things were for the good of the patients and the hospital. Bill Kaplan is my hero.

## CHAPTER FOURTEEN

# Interview with a Hero
# Bill Kaplan

## To what do you attribute your career success?

*First and foremost, my parents. But aside from my parents, I've come to realize that I have an ability to see everything—no matter what it is—as being very simple. My parents sent me into the service when I was seventeen years old. When I got out of the service, I started a business. I didn't have the education to do anything else, and I was an entrepreneur at heart. My father had been in the handbag business ... he was a salesperson, and I had worked in a handbag factory, so I learned the business starting at the bottom and knew everything there was to know about the product. When it was time to expand my business, to get new customers, I went after J.C. Penney and Sears. They had lots of salespeople calling on them, but I knew more about the product than anyone else, and my customers loved giving me business. I kept it all very simple and ultimately, we became the second-largest handbag manufacturer in the Unites States.*

## Philanthropy has become a way of life for you. Where does your philanthropic drive come from?

*Again … my parents. I owe so much to my parents—to my father for his genius and my mother for her unwavering emotional support. My father's philosophy was based on the idea that there are no bad people, only bad circumstances. He used to say, "Don't criticize people. How do you know what you would do in their circumstances? It's easy to be a great guy when everything is going your way, but if your luck were to change, do you really know how you would behave?"*

*My father was a generous man who cared about society as a whole. He gave to his own synagogue, but he also gave to the Greek Orthodox and Catholic churches in town. He and my mother used to buy toys all year long. At Chanukah, he spread them out in the basement of my parents' home and hung up a sign saying "Papa Louie's Toy Store." He asked my daughters to invite their Jewish friends to the house so they could choose a gift. Then, at Christmas, he told my daughters to invite their Christian friends to come to the house and select a gift.*

*I have very fond memories of my father, and knowing that I'm living out his philosophy makes my philanthropic activities all the more meaningful to me. Giving to others has brought deep joy into my life. My philanthropy has been local, in the city of Newburgh, New York. I've given a good deal of time, energy, and money to the city, but I know in my heart that I've gotten back far more than I've given.*

## In addition to being a philanthropist, Eric describes you as a visionary. Do you agree?

*Yes and no. Yes, I have good ideas, and having a vision is critical, so I guess I'm a visionary. But, a lot of people have good ideas. Implementation is everything. You can't just think about what you want to do. You have to take action and implement.*

## Can you say a bit more about taking action and implementing?

*In business as well as in philanthropy, I'm a great believer in prompt action. I've never advocated recklessness, but I've always been acutely aware that windows of opportunity can close very quickly. With the right support, at the right moment in time, a non-profit organization can go on to flourish for decades into the future. I've seen*

*this happen again and again. Rather than waiting for every conceivable doubt to be re-
solved, I favor acting swiftly and then making any needed adjustments as time unfolds.*

*My dear friend, Dick Bauer, shares my philosophy. He says, "Imperfect action is
better than perfect inaction."*

*Eric said that when you were chairman of St. Luke's, you had a great ability to
galvanize the members of the board. How did you do that?*

*I did the same at St. Luke's as I did with my own business when I was a young
man: I learned from the bottom up. By the time I was chairman of St. Luke's, I
had been on every committee (over a fifteen-year period) and knew every detail of the
hospital. I had more knowledge and I shared that knowledge with the board members.*

**Eric was very young when he joined St. Luke's. What gave you con-
fidence in Eric and prompted you to back him in his endeavors?**

*I probably saw a bit of myself in Eric; we matched: Eric had an entrepreneurial
mind like me. He also had vision and the ability to implement, to take the necessary
action to achieve the vision. Eric was a bright young guy and got to work immediately
to turn the hospital around. It was obvious that he was using St. Luke's as a stepping
stone—it wasn't a permanent position for him—so that was a motivating factor for him.*

*Eric's greatest contribution to St. Luke's was the hospice. I tried to get the hospice
in Newburgh, and it didn't work out. I had been out to dinner with a member of the
health care community in New York City, and during our dinner, he told me they had
just opened the first hospice in New York. I knew nothing about hospice then, but it
just so happened that my sister-in-law had recently died of cancer. We helped take care
of her and it was a terrible thing to watch: She was living in her apartment and it was
impossible to get the right kind of care for her. She was so fragile and in constant pain.
When I heard how hospice helps, all I could think of was how wonderful it would
have been if we'd had that kind of care for my sister-in-law. I immediately went to
the board of St. Luke's and said we needed to get a hospice program in Newburgh,
and they agreed. We applied to the government, and were vying for the government
assistance with Middletown, about thirty miles away. Newburgh lost to Middletown
after a very long battle.*

**Eric knew how disappointed I was. He came in my office one day
and asked, "Mr. Kaplan, do you really want this hospice program?"**

*"YES!" I replied without hesitating.*

*That was all he needed. He set out, determined to bring this hospice program to St. Luke's—and he did. I don't know how in the world he did it, but instead of Middletown getting the funds for their own hospice, we ended up with a hospice that was for both Middletown and Newburgh. We wouldn't have had the hospice program in Newburgh without Eric, and it's been a great asset to the community.*

*After that, Eric moved on. I would have given anything to keep him at St. Luke's.*

## Did you realize the impact you had on Eric?

*No. I certainly realized how talented Eric was, and his impact on St. Luke's, but I had no idea of my impact on him. I think as we go through life, we don't necessarily realize the impact we have on others.*

## CHAPTER FIFTEEN

# Allowing Others to Be Successful
# Jim Dalton

My commitment with HCA (to turn around St. Luke's) was nearing an end. They wanted me to stay and enticed me with more money and more benefits, but I knew I'd no longer be content running a single hospital: I wanted to work *harder, faster, stronger*—and be better than anyone else. It was my turn to become a multi-hospital guy. I still had that chip on my shoulder, the fear of failure and accompanying need to prove myself—even though at a young age, I had achieved more than I probably ever dreamed I would.

I received a call from HCA asking if I'd be interested in a position in Pittsburgh. Carolyn and I had lived in Pittsburgh while I was getting my master's degree and swore we'd never return: We were poor then, didn't particularly like Pittsburgh, and now had no interest in going backward. But, I was excited about the possible position, so we decided to make a trip to Pittsburgh to check things out: We had a great long weekend there; I accepted the position and became the youngest regional vice president in Hospital Corporation of America, the largest hospital management company in the world. At the time, they didn't have any facilities in Pittsburgh; I opened offices there and started managing two hospitals. Once again that chip on my shoulder was to my benefit as I proved to myself—and everyone else—just how good I was: Six years later, I oversaw fifteen hospitals, all with the highest profit margins in the company.

Unfortunately, I wasn't inspired by the company president at the time: He was reserved, extremely conservative, very slow moving, and unexciting ... at least to me. Under his direction, the company was exceptionally bureaucratic and boring. When my profit margins were sky high, I took risks and started to push back against the president—and the status quo. In fact, I went out on a limb quite a few times to the point where I should have had my head examined. I was never nasty or negative, but I was very "in your face" to the president. I tried to break up the status quo every chance I got. I knew I was the youngest regional vice president and also the highest performing, but I was certain I wasn't the highest paid. As I've mentioned, having a lot of money was never something I focused on, but my earnings were a barometer for me and I constantly pushed the edge for more money. One year the president gave me a tremendous evaluation, but then I got a lousy increase. We weren't in the same location (he was in Nashville and I was in Pittsburgh), so when I saw the small raise in my paycheck, I gave him a call.

"Gee, with all due respect, it's really not enough," I said.

"Well Eric, you've had numerous increases and whether you know it or not you're the highest paid regional vice president and you're at the top of the pay scale. The board won't allow an additional increase," he replied.

"Well, I'm not happy. Is there something we can do about it?" I asked, while thinking to myself that I could just go elsewhere.

A couple of days later, he called me back and said, "Eric, you're so important to this company. We understand your concern, so I'm coming up there with our vice president of personnel and we'd like to meet with you over the next couple of days. Let's go out for dinner, let's build a vision together, and we'll talk about things."

And I said, "Gee, I appreciate that and I think highly of the vice president of personnel. But if you're going to spend four days here, that trip will cost ten thousand dollars with airfare for the two of you, hotels, meals and a rental car."

"Yes, it probably will, Eric, but you are that important to this company," he answered.

"Well," I suggested, "why don't you stay in Nashville and just send me the ten thousand and we'll call it even?" I replied very seriously and without sarcasm.

It was akin to telling my dad years before that I intended to sell my textbooks and go to the Bahamas. It made sense to me, but it sent my dad through the roof. This particular president was a low-key kind of guy; he didn't go through the roof, but I can imagine what he was thinking. He and the VP of personnel did come up to Pittsburgh—but I didn't get a bigger increase.

About three years into my tenure as division vice president with HCA, many members of management (me included) decided to buy the company. There were approximately three hundred investors—including management members and venture capitalists—who participated in the endeavour. We privatized the company, changed the name to Quorum, and decided it was time for new leadership. Jim Dalton, a regional vice president for a hospital management company, was brought in as the new president. Jim was a no-nonsense, straightforward, unyielding guy who was also honest, ethical and charismatic. In my book, he was the Richie Moran of business. I still recall my first conversation with Jim after his appointment as president.

"You're doing a hell of a job here," he said, "and I'm giving you carte blanche to do even more. I recognize the problems and the bureaucracy we have. I'm worried about both and want to make some changes, but it's going to take a long time. I want you to promise me that if anybody in our company gets in your way, you'll call me immediately and in turn, I promise you I'll take care of whatever it is in a New York minute."

I probably had a big grin covering my entire face. It was like music to my ears. The previous president was a wonderful, ethical guy, but a boring leader. With Jim Dalton at the helm, I felt I'd been saved from the doldrums of do-nothingness. And not only was I saved from boredom, but I was given the liberty to implement changes that positively impacted many people.

Jim Dalton kept his commitment—to me and to Quorum. He was faced with changing the culture of an organization that provided services to more than two hundred hospitals, many of them non-profit, and many of them with a multitude of boards and varied needs. Under Jim's leadership, I became even more successful. As an organization, we had always focussed on educating non-profit boards, of which we had hundreds. I took the carte blanche given to me by Jim and started an educational program called Foundations for the Future for all our non-profit boards. It was the first time anything like this had ever been done: I planned a three-day symposium, brought in nationally-known speakers, and set up a trustee forum. I invited my division of twenty hospitals and then opened it up to the boards of directors in the rest of HCA. Board chairmen from around the country came to my district to learn how to be better board members. It was a phenomenal event. However, when you perform *harder, faster, stronger*, and better, it doesn't always sit well with your peers, and it certainly didn't sit well with mine at the time. Long-standing vice presidents started to talk, and what they had to say wasn't complimentary. Through it all, however, Jim Dalton backed me, even though he had his own difficulties. In fact, he was the opening speaker for the three-day symposium.

I constantly questioned the status quo; Jim never put the brakes on me, though he never openly condoned my style—at least not to me directly—until we attended an HCA national convention together. My wife Carolyn and I had the pleasure of sitting next to Dr. Tom Frist Sr., the founder of Quorum, and his wife. I admired the Frists—they were wonderful people—and I believe Dr. Frist created one of the most positive corporate cultures in the world at that time.

After dinner, Carolyn and I were talking with a couple of colleagues when we were approached by Jim Dalton and Tom Frist Jr., chairman of the board and son of the founder. I'd met Tom before, but we didn't know each other well.

Then Jim turned to Tom, and said, "Tom, we're so blessed and honored to have Eric as one of our vice presidents. He's one of our best, even though he would rather plead for forgiveness than ask for permission. That's exactly the kind of guy we need."

That was one of the proudest moments of my career.

Some of the happiest times in my life were the years I spent in Pittsburgh: Carolyn and I lived in a great neighborhood; I was in the zone, a superstar running twenty hospitals, earning a lot of money and buying a lot of stock, and we had our beautiful daughter Jennifer, who was now five years old. And, I respected, admired, and learned from Jim Dalton. Jim and I often had to deal with the same issues, and while our styles were similar, Jim was far more subtle than I. Through Jim's example, I came to realize that a more restrained approach often produces better results.

Eventually, I decided I wanted different, bigger, and better things and started looking around. I was offered a contract with a large health care organization at a significantly higher salary than I was earning. It took months to negotiate my contract with this company: As much as I was ready to move on, I wasn't totally ready to leave Quorum, or Jim Dalton, though I accepted the job. I was executive vice-president, number three in the company, and ultimately responsible for 22,000 employees. One month into the job, an incident occurred and I became very uncomfortable with some of the company's policies and decisions. I refused to become a participant in that incident and from that moment on, I was essentially blacklisted by those above me. I was given Herculean tasks to meet earnings thresholds that were impossible to reach. I worked day and night for twelve months and when we announced earnings, I missed the mark by one cent a share—and got fired because of it. Another face plant. But, in reality, I didn't get fired because of missing earnings by one penny per share; I got fired because I was different and I let people know it, which was political stupidity in many ways. But, it was the right thing to do: I was not about to take part in practices with which I was uncomfortable. I had a fantastic severance agreement, which resulted in me leaving the company with a lot of money. I started looking for work and placed a call to Jim Dalton.

"It's got to be right; I'm up to my ears in alligators here," Jim said. "I don't want to bring you in and feed you to the alligators that I'm fighting. Give me some time."

"No problem," I replied, a bit disappointed. I would have loved to work for Jim again, but I respected his honesty and straightforwardness.

I took me six months to find the right job. On a Wednesday morning, I accepted a position as senior vice president of operations of a multi-hospital company in Atlanta. That afternoon, I received a call from Jim Dalton offering me a position back with Quorum.

"There's nothing I wouldn't do to work with you again, Jim. But I've just accepted another job and I can't go against my word to the people I've just committed to," I answered.

Jim and I were both disappointed, but we've remained friends ever since. I moved my family to Atlanta, and Jim embarked on a program to change the culture of an anaemic, non-energetic organization to a vital, fast-moving entrepreneurial machine—and he succeeded.

He continued with Quorum for several more years before moving on, and served on a number of corporate boards. Jim Dalton stood up for what was right. At times, he put himself in jeopardy for the enrichment and betterment of his employees. He provided excitement, challenge, and fun—and supported me in becoming a winner.

He was strategic and to the point, low-key, matter-of-fact, and pragmatic. He had warmth and sympathy coupled with the ability to get the job done, very similar to Richie Moran and Tom Horton. These guys got the job done, and they got it done while being assertive, but with style and charisma. Jim Dalton was a shining superstar and my hero—of which there were few—in my business career.

## CHAPTER SIXTEEN

# Interview with a Hero
# Jim Dalton

### How do you define success and what leads to success?

*Success is tied into achieving the type of life you prescribe for yourself. I've always described success as reaching as close to your full potential as you can, both personally and professionally. I imagine for a moment that I'm confronting the mythical pearly gates and am asked the question, "What would you change?" ... if I can look back and say "damn little," then I'd say that's been a successful life.*

*The most successful people I've known in my career are driven, and I think the drive for success is purely internal: I always believed that no one can put any more pressure on me than I put on myself, and I can't put any more pressure on others than they put on themselves. The environment in which people find themselves can have an influence on their success: some environments are enabling while others are suppressing. I've seen people who are guilty of under-optimizing in an environment that would have encouraged or allowed them to optimize their personal attributes. Successful people take advantage of their own internal pressures; they are driven toward continuous improvement, to be successful and to allow the people around them be successful.*

*Honesty and integrity also play a significant role in success. To me, if a person is honest—with himself and others—then he will have a greater chance at success.*

*I've known people who are highly successful financially, yet unhappy. Money in the bank does not equal success. If you're not satisfied with who you are and what you're striving to accomplish, then you are not successful.*

**You said, "Successful people allow those around them to be successful." Can you elaborate?**

*I can spend a short period of time with someone and form judgments in terms of how they relate to others, and how driven they are. Many people are strongly driven, but for the wrong reasons—purely personal reasons. If I'm with someone for fifteen minutes and nine out of ten sentences begin with the word "I," then I know that individual is more concerned for himself than anything else. I've seen corporate executives speak at investor conferences, inferring they are personally responsible for everything that happened in that organization. That's a turnoff to me.*

**Eric uses a number of adjectives to describe you: no nonsense, straightforward, and unyielding—combined with honesty and integrity. Can you talk about integrity, and where your integrity stems from?**

*As an aside, the way Eric describes me is a really good description of the way I view him. I think he knew I'd do what I told him I would do, and he knew what I told him was the truth. I'm not sure he knew that instinctively from the beginning, but we grew to feel the same way about each other. Maybe we had more in common than we realized at the time.*

*Integrity has always been important to me. If people do not respect you for your integrity, they won't respect you at all. The further one goes in an organization, the more critical integrity becomes. I learned it from my parents: They instilled in me very early that I should treat everyone with respect, and deal honestly with people, and I've tried to instill the same values in our nine children. It sounds old fashioned, but it's amazing how often the "do unto others as you would have done unto you" approach works. I highly respected one of the founders of the company Eric and I worked for. He was the walking, talking, living conscience of the company. So many times I heard him say, "If you ever have any doubt as to whether something is best for the company or best for the patient, always choose the patient—and likewise with the employees." I've repeated that many times to people.*

## What does "hero" mean to you, and who have been your heroes? Did you seek out your heroes or did they find you?

*A hero is in the eye of the beholder. One person's hero might be another's dunce. I've had many heroes; I've been fortunate pretty much every step of the way to find someone who took an interest in me, and created an environment that allowed me to branch out. I started working in the family business, a variety store, when I was in the third grade. When I was fifteen years old, I had my first job outside the family, working as a radio disc jockey. It was a bold move for someone to put me in front of a microphone at age fifteen, and it gave me a lot of confidence. I guess that person was one of my heroes.*

*When I was getting into hospital administration, I sought to do a residency at a particular hospital because I'd heard so many good things about one individual and his management style. I went to that hospital with the thought that I'd be there for one year, and I ended up staying for five years. My grad school colleagues had been right: This individual was the one who picked me up and spun me on my way when I was trying to decide what it meant to be a hospital administrator. He had a tremendous influence on me and I consider him a hero. I've had some remarkable influences along the way: In our careers we need different people at different times—different kicks in the backside to get us moving.*

## Describe Eric and your relationship with him when he worked in your organization.

*Eric never reported directly to me: I was recruited to be CEO of HCA Management Company and at the time, Eric was a regional vice president. One of the early things I did was to visit the group offices: I spent time with each of our regional vice presidents, getting to know them, understanding their attitudes and management philosophies, and what they hoped to achieve with the company. Eric was a standout in that group of people in terms of his perception of his job, the company, and where he was trying to go with his group. He was a very dynamic leader at a very young age. He also stood out because he was a contrarian and didn't mind disagreeing with the bureaucracy. The company was going through a phase in which different management philosophies were being established—some that people liked and felt comfortable with, and others people didn't like, but neglected to challenge. Eric never missed an opportunity to challenge, and I liked that. I found that people in the corporate office were somewhat intimidated by Eric; perhaps they didn't understand what he was trying to accomplish, plus the company had been slow-moving and Eric was impatient. And again, I liked that because I was impatient also. Every time Eric came to the corporate office, his reverberation was felt for several days after he left. It was great.*

*It's amazing how much you can learn if you'll give people an opportunity to open up and tell you what's good, what's bad, and what's somewhere in the middle. Eric was very forthcoming with his observations. He saw all kinds of opportunities we could take advantage of—if we created a little more flexibility. He and I plotted together without even knowing it. We created a fraternity of sorts—a group of people who wanted to challenge the status quo.*

*Eric is one of the most driven individuals I ever met in my career: He was driven to go above and beyond what was required of him, constantly trying to improve both himself and his organization. At the same time, he was very good at enabling people around him, expecting more of them than what they might have expected of themselves, and allowing them to be successful. Eric was a game changer. He was personally aggressive—always wanting to expand his career opportunities—and that type of leadership can create a very positive environment if people know that you mean it.*

## How do people know you mean it?

*Through your actions. There's no other way. If you truly measure your own success by the success of those around you, that word gets around, and people will migrate to that organization. I'm proud to say that has happened many times in my own life. I've had people come up to me ten years after they've worked in our company and say, "All these years, I've been looking for another company like that one, and I just want you to know I never found it." There's not a more heartwarming thing someone can say to an old CEO than "Hey, we had a pretty good thing there." I've also had people say, "I had no idea how great our company was until I tried to replicate it in another location." That's the pinnacle of success.*

**Eric said you sometimes put yourself in jeopardy for the betterment of your employees. How do you see that relating to the achievement of long-term success?**

*It never occurred to me to go the other way, to risk one of our associates for my betterment. It ties into integrity and respect for the individual. You encourage your people to take risks and make decisions on their own, and then you stand behind them whether they're right or wrong. You build their confidence, but at the same time you're risking your own career. The least you can do is to stand behind the people who are on the front lines every day. They are the ones helping the customers and trying to make the company a better one. If they're wrong, then help them find a way to make it right.*

*When you walk into roles like those Eric and I had at Quorum, you put your job on the line the day you arrive. You can decide to do the job with integrity and the make the tough decisions, or you can decide to take no risks at all—to do everything possible just to hold on to that job. Those who make the latter decision are the ones who lose.*

**Eric talked about the way you took the organization from being slow-moving and not very dynamic to a smooth-running, highly successful entrepreneurial machine. How did you do that? What qualities do you see in yourself that helped you make that change?**

*First of all, I didn't do it. I was fortunate to be in the CEO role, presiding over the game. We had so much talent in the company; we hired good people and let them know they could self-optimize in the organization if they wanted to. We wanted to create an environment that allowed people to self-optimize, as opposed to being cookie-cutters. We didn't give them a bunch of rules; in fact, we threw out a lot of rules that had been around for a long time. I tried to identify the people who could help lead the business forward, and we did need to replace a few people. We had a lot of meetings and did a lot of talking. We were growing extremely rapidly which gave us the opportunity to try new things, even if we made a few mistakes along the way.*

*I took some fairly rigid positions and made some people very unhappy during that period of time. I think the thing that helped me was that I was consistent and I wasn't trying to achieve any personal fame or gain: I was simply trying to get my job done.*

*I didn't take that company anywhere. I happened to be the presiding officer over a heck of a team.*

## Did you realize that you had such an impact on Eric?

*No. Eric and I didn't spend that much time together one on one. Except for a couple of comments here and there, I believe the first time I heard that Eric considered me to be a positive influence on him was after he left the company. But I think we always knew it in terms of our communication: We always communicated with respect, and never argued. On the company organizational chart, there were probably three people between him and me, but I answered my own phone, and Eric knew he could pick up the phone and call me anytime.*

*Eric's never been a patronizing individual, so I didn't get any warm and fuzzy signals from him. We simply had easy, direct communication with one another, and I believe he appreciated the help I was trying to give him.*

*I think one of the reasons Eric might say I had an unusual impact on him was he had an unusual impact on me. A manager, a president, a leader, a CEO, is simply a reflection of all the people around him. Eric's one of those people who really gave me a lot of energy and a lot of hope.*

## CHAPTER SEVENTEEN

# A Huge Mistake

When I was offered the job in Atlanta, Carolyn and I decided it would be a good move for the family: Jennifer had another six years in school, and it would give her the stability of being in the same school environment the entire time. Two and a half years later, I moved on to another organization in Atlanta, a large multi-faceted health care company where I stayed for five years, until 2000, when I was able to negotiate a generous severance package, a true golden parachute.

In 1995, Carolyn and I had purchased six acres of land on the coast of Maine, with a vision of building our dream home and retiring there when I turned fifty. During the five years prior to my retirement, we worked with the town, the state, designers, and a builder, and ultimately built the home of our dreams: Our own private road ambled down to the house, a John Calvin Stevens gray shingle-style home with a magnificent rear porch overlooking the Atlantic Ocean, the waves crashing on the rocks only fifty feet away. It was something you'd see in a magazine.

We moved into our new home in the month of May after Jennifer graduated from high school. As we were unpacking, Carolyn discovered the letter I had written fifteen years prior, and we sat down and read the details of the vision I had created for our future. Our lives were exactly as I had described in my letter, from our beautiful home to the exact amount of money we had in the bank. Reading that letter with the love of my life by my side, and seeing that we were living my dream, renewed my faith in God and the fact that there is something bigger and better out there—something influencing my life on a spiritual level. At that moment, I was grateful to God for the people he put in my path: my heroes, who helped me achieve my dreams.

In late May, we planted petunias, geraniums, and all the typical New England annuals. It was a beautiful spring and a beautiful life. I filled my time with back-to-nature-type activities and even did some of the major landscaping around the house. It wasn't easy, however, to break into the Maine coast culture. I was a wealthy fifty-year-old and a conservative, and I had very little in common with the locals.

Retiring at age fifty was a poignant experience: I'd been operating at full tilt for thirty years and now, the highlight of my day was walking along our three-quarter-mile dirt road to the mailbox. I was doing just that on a spectacular late-August afternoon, accompanied by our white lab, Scooter. The sun, slightly obscured by the myriad of trees on our property, was already beginning to move toward the west, and the birch leaves were vibrating in the breeze. It was idyllic, like a French impressionistic painting. I was about one hundred feet from the mailbox when I had an epiphany of sorts—another *Sittin' on the Dock on the Bay* moment—accompanied by a sinking feeling in the pit of my stomach, and thought to myself, *What in the hell have I done? This isn't working for me. I've made a huge mistake! I have to get out of here!*

Scooter and I walked back to the house. I was anxious to share my revelation with Carolyn.

"There you go again," she said. "Will you ever be happy?"

I was fifty-one years old. Carolyn and I had been together for thirty-eight years. She was always a willing supporter of everything I did—but not this time. It was only the second time in our relationship that she ever pushed back on me.

Not two months later, stormy seas raged once again: the stock market tanked and I instantaneously lost fifty percent of my net worth. And then, my golden parachute—that I had so deftly negotiated—blew up because the board of directors of my former employer decided to declare bankruptcy and take the business under … and with it, my severance package.

Carolyn and I decided to sell our dream home and move—but not far. We put our home on the market and I started to look for a new job. It's amazing how quickly grapes turn to vinegar after you leave your career: I hadn't kept in touch with any of my contacts because I thought I was done—after all, I had retired. The job search wasn't easy. I decided to do consulting work in Dallas, Texas for a former associate who was then the CEO of a health care company that was experiencing some difficulties. I agreed to help him for sixty days, and ended up commuting from Camden, Maine to Dallas, Texas every week for eighteen months. My life consisted of getting up at 3:00 a.m. every Monday, going to whatever airport was not snowed out and flying to Boston, where I connected to the American Airlines flight to Dallas. I arrived in Dallas at noon and went directly to the office. I worked in the office until eight or nine o'clock every night. On Friday mornings, I got up at 4:30 a.m. to make the trek back to Camden. I was always on the 6 a.m. flight out of Dallas, which arrived in Boston late morning. When that flight arrived on time, I was able to catch a pre-noon connecting flight to Rockland, Maine; but, if my flight from Dallas arrived late, I had to wait around in Boston until the 4:30 p.m. flight to Rockland, which was often delayed. There were many times when I didn't walk into my house until eight o'clock in the evening.

A year and a half of commuting back and forth to Dallas was all I could handle and I was happy to be back in Maine, though our home hadn't yet sold and I was trying to figure out what's next? When my career was in full-swing, I always had the answer to that question in the back of my mind; however, this time I wasn't so sure.

Another spring came, accompanied by the northern New England mud season. It was 2003. On a cold April afternoon, I trudged through the mud, taking my daily walk up our dirt driveway to pick up the mail. I noticed an odd-shaped envelope, hand-addressed to Carolyn.

When I got back to the house, I handed the envelope to Carolyn, and she pulled out a letter that began, "Dear Mrs. Rieseberg, I am Kimberly's biological mother." It had been nineteen years since Kimberly passed away. Carolyn and I sat down and read the letter together. It continued, "I have never stopped thinking about Kimberly: every one of her birthdays, when she graduated from kindergarten, junior high, and high school. I wonder if she went to college. I have respected your wishes over the years not to contact you or Kimberly, but I just need to know how she is." Carolyn, my rock, stable through thick and thin, broke down and wept.

"We're going to call her," I said, taking Carolyn by the arm and leading her to my home office. Within a few minutes, I found the phone number and dialed. I was taken by surprise when a man answered. I didn't want to create any problems by revealing something I shouldn't.

"Is Maggie there?" I asked.

"No, she's out shopping," was the reply.

"This is Eric Rieseberg. We just received a letter," I said.

"I know about the letter," he interrupted.

Relieved, I took a deep breath and continued, "Carolyn and I read Maggie's letter and want to let you know that Kimberly died nineteen years ago, one day before her fourth birthday."

The man on the other end of the phone let out a wail of uncontrolled agony, and then began to cry. Carolyn and I listened, our hearts breaking, while this man told us he was not the biological father, but he knew about the child and had married Kimberly's biological mother. As we were talking, Maggie returned from shopping to see her husband crying on the telephone.

"It's Eric and Carolyn Rieseberg," he told his wife as he handed her the phone. Carolyn was sitting right next to me, but I had the phone in my hand, so I explained to Maggie what had happened. When she burst into tears, I crumbled from the inside out. My dear wife took the phone from my hand and I stepped away. Carolyn and Maggie talked for a half hour. I never asked what they talked about, but I have no doubt Carolyn did her best to console Maggie, one mother to another.

OOO

It took three years to sell our home. Meanwhile, my entrepreneurial spirit took over, and I decided to undertake a new venture, and started a hospital company with some fellow associates. The business took off like a rocket ship, but in the end, I endured another face plant.

## CHAPTER EIGHTEEN

# My Ultimate Hero

The best thing I ever did was to marry my wife.

Carolyn Jean Salerno Rieseberg—God's gift to the world, with a smile that lit up any room she walked into.

I was nineteen years old when I met Carolyn, a month after my spring break trip to the Bahamas. I was in a bar with a buddy of mine and Carolyn was in an adjacent booth. She was of Dutch and Italian heritage and her looks portrayed the best of both: blond hair and blue eyes, dark skin. She was wearing a tan striped blouse, her hair in pigtails, and her dark Coppertone tan highlighted her beautiful white teeth and contagious smile. *Woweee!* I thought to myself. She pulled out a cigarette and started searching for a match. I scurried to find a book of matches, and then tossed it to her, hitting her left shoulder. We chatted for a while and I asked for her phone number.

"Look it up," she said, with a warm but challenging smile.

Salerno was a very common name in Port Washington, a hamlet on the north shore of Long Island. Over the next few days, I went through quite a few Salernos before finally finding Carolyn and asking her for a date.

Carolyn had a beautiful personality: she was warm, kind, and stable as a rail car. As heroes are, she was a strong—yet subtle—guide throughout my life, in ways that I'm still discovering. She is the one and only person I have ever completely trusted.

The oldest of four siblings, Carolyn came from a working class family: Her dad, a heroic veteran of World War II, was in the landscaping business. She was very bright and wanted to go to college, but her dad was opposed, so she went to secretarial school in New York City instead, and then landed a job at NBC at Rockefeller Center, working for the vice president of public relations. Two and a half years into our relationship, Carolyn decided to leave home, and along with two girlfriends she moved to Pennsylvania and attended Penn State University part time. Six months later, I asked her to marry me.

When I went to grad school in Pittsburgh, Carolyn got a job on the sixth floor at the University of Pittsburgh School of Public Health. We walked together in the mornings, me to grad school and Carolyn to her job, and had lunch together every day. We were dirt poor: We drank powdered milk and stole salt, pepper, and sugar from the school cafeteria—but we made it through. I graduated and got my first job.

Carolyn decided to go back to college to study geriatric fitness when Jennifer was in elementary school. At her graduation, when she stepped on stage to accept her degree (with a 4.0 average), Jennifer and I leapt from our seats, cheering and clapping. She was our hero that day, as she was every day.

When Jennifer was in ninth grade, she made the cut and became a varsity cheerleader for the Greater Atlanta Christian School. I attended as many games as possible to support Jennifer. Carolyn was working, running fitness programs for the elderly, but she never missed a basketball or football game in three years. She was always there to support our daughter. Over the years, Jennifer told us that she appreciated her mom's consistent attendance … and as a mother to my two grandsons, she has modeled herself after Carolyn.

My wife always put her own interests after those of our daughters and me. I believe when a husband and wife put one another first, the marriage will always be successful. I did put Carolyn first, but I was on a career path—for me and for us. Carolyn always supported me with my next career move. In some ways, we had kind of a navy life … continually moving. I was continuously looking for the next big thing, even before I took my next job. Carolyn was right there with me, though, at the end of my career, I believe my rigorous vocational pursuits had become a bit onerous for her.

Happy under almost any circumstance, money was of no consequence to Carolyn. I came home one day with a very big bonus check.

"Oh … Okay," she shrugged.

Money wasn't where it was at for her, and she saw to it that we were frugal, and not materialistic. What she did value was me. When my mountain expeditions and survival training got out of hand, she influenced my decision to stop. Actually, she told me to stop. It was the first time in all our years together that she pushed back on me.

"Enough is enough. You're not doing this anymore. You've got a wife and child, and I can no longer handle wondering if you'll come home alive," she commanded.

Soon, I would be the one wondering.

After we sold our home in Maine, we moved to New Hampshire. On a freezing cold day in February of 2009, I was in Washington, D.C. pursuing my new venture when Carolyn called me:

"I just had an appointment with my gynecologist and she's referring me to another doctor. She thinks there's a chance I have ovarian cancer."

I hung up the phone and made the fastest trip back to New Hampshire from D.C. anyone has ever made.

And then the war began.

We had to go through the American health care system, a travesty I helped create. I had flashbacks of Kimberly dying of cancer. I'm the guy—the health care expert who knows where all the buttons are and how to access every resource—but it did absolutely no good. Though I knew Carolyn's disease was terminal more often than not, I couldn't admit it to myself. If I did, I would have lost my edge. Carolyn and I were fighting to win, and I was determined to sustain the tremendously high level of energy needed to wage war. My wife fought her disease like a true hero—enduring surgery, weeks of chemo followed by a break, and then more chemo, dealing with hospitals, their bureaucracy, and even mistakes. And then waiting, hoping, and praying for clear CT scans. I would have fought for the rest of my life to save Carolyn's life, but the fight was not good enough.

Carolyn Jean Salerno Rieseberg passed away in December of 2010, after a nearly two-year battle.

There are times when we know in our hearts that the war cannot be won ... but we continue to fight because the alternative is unthinkable. We cannot admit defeat, and the ultimate loss comes far too soon.

Even though I knew it was coming, the moment of Carolyn's death was a complete surprise to me.

## CHAPTER NINETEEN

# The Reckoning

In the spring of 2013, nearly three years after Carolyn's death, I started to feel like myself again. The dark curtains of grief finally started to part. I ended up making three trips to the northeast during the course of seven months: a reunion, a "coming home," and a Manhasset Lacrosse Hall of Fame installation. First, I attended a Manhasset Booster Club Hall of Fame reunion, during which my old lacrosse team members and I were honored on the field at the Manhasset versus Chaminade lacrosse game, a seasonal highlight. It was great to be reunited with my old team-mates as I hadn't seen most of them for almost forty-five years. During dinner, each of the senior varsity players gave a brief speech. My turn finally came ...

"Gentlemen, I'm honored by your presence and your support of my being here. I want to thank you all—and I need to thank *you*, Renzie—for showing me the way. Being kicked off the team was the biggest wakeup call of my young life. And then, two weeks after I left the lacrosse team, the love of my life and I broke up. You all went on to become Long Island champions."

And then, looking directly at Renzie, I said, "Interestingly enough, the girlfriend that dropped me is happily married, lives in Manhasset, and her son actually played for you at Williams College. His name isn't important. But what is important is that because I was no longer with her, I met the *true* love of my life, Carolyn. She has passed away, but we were together for thirty-eight wonderful years of marriage. It couldn't have been better. I'm very happy and honored to be with you guys."

I received a warm round of applause. The reunion gave my teammates and I a few great days that rekindled some wonderful memories, and our team was invited back in November to be installed in the Manhasset Lacrosse Hall of Fame.

That summer, I decided to take a road trip from Florida to the northeast. That's when I reconnected with old friends, plus Richie Moran and Bill Kaplan. I guess it was a "coming home" of sorts.

The Manhasset Booster Club Hall of Fame installation in November recognized our 1967 varsity team for its undefeated 18-0 season as Long Island champions. All the members of our team—myself included—stood on the platform for the installation. Renzie stood in front of us and gave a short speech. He said we were the best crop of athletes he'd ever coached in thirty-two years.

During the reception at a well-known Manhasset watering hole, Bob Rule, our goalie and American Lacrosse Hall of Fame member, approached me—with Renzie at his side—and made an announcement in front of the entire team.

"You know what I'm doing next week?" he asked, with a huge smile on his face.

"I'm getting your name engraved on our Long Island Championship trophy. Coach Lamb here has approved this whole thing." I glanced at Renzie. He was smiling, but silent. I suspect his mind was revisiting the past.

Bob went on to say that Renzie and the whole team had agreed that my name and number should be put on the trophy. "This trophy belongs to you as much as it belongs to anyone else."

I jested that perhaps my number on the trophy should be 15/18ths—instead of 56, my jersey number—which resulted in some good-natured chuckles.

The recognition that it was my trophy as well as theirs was a wonderful tribute. We all hugged manly hugs. Somehow, with the recognition of Bob and Renzie, the act of many years ago no longer made a difference. We were once again a team.

# Seek a Hero. Be a Hero.

We're all just one lab report away from disaster. None of us is immune to pain and very few of us get through life without enduring rough waters. It's how we endure the stormy seas that matters. Pain comes in many and sundry packages. When Carolyn and I realized we would likely lose our three-year-old daughter to cancer, the pain was unimaginable. How could we continue to live? How could we carry on without Kimberly?

Three days before Kimberly passed away, the president of the medical staff where our daughter was hospitalized asked if he could talk with me. We met in a library area of the hospital—a quiet, musty old place with leather furniture. We spent an hour together, and he shared that he'd lost all five members of his family over the span of fifteen years: Each of his four children and his wife of many years had all passed away at different times, from an accident, while serving our country, or from an illness. I knew right then and there that I wasn't the only one who had to cope with stormy seas: this man was dealing with even worse circumstances than I. *If he was able to survive and flourish, then I sure as hell could!*

Just as the stormy seas and face plants of our lives come in different packages, so do those who help us up along the way—our heroes.

Though I didn't know the president of the medical staff well, my conversation with him was like a lightning bolt, jolting me out of my despair. And then, there are my heroes: These men all share the attributes of heroes that I laid out in chapter four:

*Heroes are ordinary people who have achieved success.*

*Heroes are consistent. Their heroic acts aren't isolated incidents.*

*Heroes are leaders.*

*Heroes work hard, even when it isn't easy.*

*Heroes set noble goals.*

*Heroes set examples others can follow.*

My heroes also happen to share a number of common traits and experiences, which I believe have shaped them into noble men:

*The military:* With one exception, my heroes were in the military, where they learned about discipline, leadership, hard work, and pushing themselves far beyond what they ever thought they could achieve.

*Marriage:* All were married, which demands loyalty, hard work, cooperation, teamwork, and goal setting. And, all were parents, a responsibility which, when done right, demands focus, communication, and character.

*Parental support:* My heroes all had good (and assuredly flawed) parents who provided support and guidance, sometimes just by example.

*Education:* Most had college educations. The one who did not benefitted from experiential education, and learned every aspect of his business from the ground up. As a result of their education, no matter what kind, my heroes all built their careers—and their reputations—from pure competency.

*Religion:* My heroes all hold to a religion; the practices, patterns, and support they derived from their respective religions helped them get through the hard times.

*Perseverance:* My heroes each endured his share of stormy seas and face plants. But, they managed to navigate the rough waters, and to get up when they were knocked down. They persevered.

OOO

We all endure stormy seas and face plants throughout our lives. I know from experience that heroes can help us to come out on the other side, and be faster, stronger, and better than we were before. Choose your heroes wisely, and you'll benefit for a lifetime, with dividends of success and happiness. *Seek a hero.*

If you haven't had the opportunity to be someone's hero, I encourage you to reach out to people in need. When you encounter someone who's just sustained a face plant, help them up. When you come across someone facing stormy seas, consider that you may have a story to tell or an example to share that will help that individual navigate the rough waters. Set examples others can follow; be a leader; be consistent. *Be a hero.*

Seek a hero, and you'll navigate the stormy seas. Be a hero, and you'll help someone up from the dirt—so they can achieve success.

# Acknowledgments

After the death of my wife of 38 years, Carolyn Jean Rieseberg, in late 2010, my life as I had known it came to an abrupt end. The loving relationships and comfortable patterns I had known so very well for many years became nonexistent. The concept that life would never be the same became ingrained in my mind and the pages of my life. However, somewhere deep inside my subconscious mind lived the desire—the urge—to breathe and live again, though perhaps differently.

This book is an outcome of that need, and an effort to re-establish the patterns, concepts, and lessons learned in the past, so I can better navigate my future—one I never expected. The writing of *Heroes Alongside Us* was an opportunity to live again, to reflect upon and revisit what's truly important in life: What legacy do we leave for our loved ones and family—and how do we go about it?

There's no doubt this book would never have been written if not for the urging of my best friend of more than fifty years, Jeff Sorg. He has been with me and my family through thick and thin, births, weddings, too many funerals, the happy times, the sad. Jeff and I have been together on the lacrosse field and the field of life. For his loyalty and sage guidance I thank him.

I thank Bob Wasno, director of the Vester Marine Biology Research Laboratory operated by Florida Gulf Coast University, for his constant urging to write this book, as well as for engaging me in thoughtful, constructive discussions about the importance of athletics in the formation of positive characteristics of real men in America. Bob is forgiven for his excellence in hockey. There is no doubt that, with a little more effort, he would have made a very good lacrosse player!

I thank Paula Nickey Hope for her support and love of me during the past three years of growth and healing. Without her almost continuous companionship, "the road back" would have been much more difficult.

I thank Pastor Todd Weston for his support, insight, and contributions to this book.

And finally, I would like to acknowledge my heroes who contributed greatly to the "making" of not only this man (as flawed as he may be), but thousands more like me. You taught us many things, but among the most important is to get back up after we have been knocked down. And for this and the many other gifts you have given—including giving so generously of your time to be interviewed for this book—I thank you.

# About the Author

Retired after forty years in healthcare administration, Eric Rieseberg is an active sportsman, sailor, certified scuba diver, and avid traveler. His favorite roles, however, are father of an exceptional daughter, and grandfather of two young grandsons—whom he hopes are future lacrosse players. Eric lives in Naples, Florida.

Eric can be reached via his website: www.HeroesAlongsideUs.com.